Contents

Acknowledgements

The editors and publishers are grateful to the following for permission to reproduce copyright material.

Allan Mackay for *There's a Ghost in the Basement, M'lord* and *A Good Knight's Work*; Evans Brothers Ltd for *Unhand Me, Squire* by Richard Tydeman; Larry Pigram for *My Fair Macbeth, Men of Magnet* and *Tarzan and Jane*; Heinemann Educational Books Ltd for *A Villa on Venus* by Kenneth Lillington, from *The Fourth Windmill Book of One-Act Plays*; Macmillan Publishers, London and Basingstoke, for *Hijack* by Charles Wells, from the Dramascript Series edited by Guy Williams; William Morris Agency Inc for *Sorry, Wrong Number* by Lucille Fletcher; Anthony Booth for *The Sky Is Overcast*.

Whilst every care has been taken to trace and acknowledge copyright, the publishers tender their apologies for any accidental infringement where copyright has proved untraceable. They would be pleased to come to a suitable arrangement with the rightful owner in each case.

Warning

PLA
HU
AND S

Ed
Sadler, H

Illustrated b

M

First published 1980 by
THE MACMILLAN COMPANY OF AUSTRALIA PTY LTD
107 Moray Street, South Melbourne 3205
6 Clarke Street, Crows Nest 2065
Reprinted 1981 (twice), 1982, 1983 (three times), 1984, 1985, 1986,
1987 (twice), 1988

Associated companies and representatives throughout the world

National Library of Australia
cataloguing in publication data

Plays of humour and suspense.

ISBN 0 333 29944 2

1. College and school drama. 2. One-act plays,
English. I. Sadler, Rex Kevin, joint ed. II. Hayllar,
Thomas Albert S., joint ed. III. Powell, Clifford
J., joint ed. IV. Baldwin, Bruce, illus.

822'.041

Set in Baskerville and Helvetica
The Markby Group, Melbourne
Printed in Hong Kong

Preface

The chuckle, the outright laugh at the clever, compelling humour; or the delicious 'wait for it' feeling that whips a class into situations of daring and danger . . . both kinds of play keep the student on mental tiptoe in *Plays of Humour and Suspense*.

In a sense it's instant drama. The plays have been chosen or written *because* they move along briskly, *because* they need very few props and *because* they can be performed, script in hand, at a moment's notice. In other words, they 'work' in the classroom. So, without further delay — let's act on it!

There's a Ghost in the Basement, M'lord

Allan Mackay

Introduction

If this comedy is given full production, as ideally it should be, much of its effect will depend upon the costuming and make-up of the 'ghostly' characters. With the exception of the skeleton, this should not provide much difficulty. The ransacking of old clothes baskets, plus some expertly applied greasepaint, will produce quite respectable spectres. The skeleton can be made up of cardboard cut-outs over a completely black costume. If a black light is available, the treating of the cut-outs with a luminous paint produces quite a devastating effect. Black walls are a great help. General stage lighting, too, is very important to give a ghostly atmosphere. Care should also be taken with the stage setting. It should be decorated in sombre colours and liberally hung with cobwebs, tattered curtains, etc.

The pace of the play is quite leisurely, accelerating at the end as events reach their climax.

Cast

Cobby the Con	A professional burglar
Siddy the Squizz	His partner in crime
Blud	The Butler of Mudslow Manor
Lord Reginald Freckleby	The owner of Mudslow Manor
Lady Freckleby	His wife
Priscilla	Their niece
Robin Hood **Napoleon Bonaparte** **Dr Frank N. Stein**	Departed guests of the Manor
Inspector Hoam **Sergeant Watkins**	Policemen
The Monster	A handy character

SCENE

A dusty, neglected room in Mudslow Manor, an apparently deserted old mansion. Cobwebs hang everywhere and the dust is thick over furniture and floor. The walls are of a very dark colour, preferably black. One door leads out to the yard and this is in the left wall, at the back. Downstage from this are heavily draped windows with a long bellpull hanging beside them. In the middle of the room, facing right is a large armchair covered with a sheet. A staircase comes down into the room from the right. Downstage from this is a 'statue', draped also with a sheet and with its back to the audience. In the back wall is a closet, its door slightly ajar. To the left of it is a large grandfather clock, its hands showing nearly midnight. Paintings, sombre and dusty, adorn the walls. Other sundry furnishings, chairs, tables, etc., can be used but they are not important for the action of the play.

*As the play begins, the stage is dimly lit, indicating that the clock is keeping the correct time. Sounds of a violent storm can be heard from time to time, and especially when the outer door is opened. It opens now with a loud creak, as **Cobby** and **Siddy**, two burglars, creep into the room. They both wear caps with half-length coats over striped jerseys. **Siddy**, bringing up the rear, carries an ancient and bulky bag containing the tools of their trade. He shivers – whether from cold or fear it is hard to tell. He closes the door after him and they tiptoe cautiously into the centre of the room.*

The time is the present.

Siddy   Lor, spare me days, Cobby — let's get out of here!

Cobby   Be quiet, Siddy.

Siddy   I gotta talk to keep me teeth from screamin'.

Cobby   Would you rather stay out in the storm with the police snapping at your heels?

Siddy   No, no, Cobby, I didn't mean that. It's just . . . . this place . . .

Cobby   What about it?

Siddy   It gives me the proper creeps all up and down me backbone. I feel like we're being watched — eyes everywhere, big bloodshot eyes, spooky eyes . . .

(He looks around fearfully.)

Cobby   You're dreaming, Siddy. This is a perfect spot for a hideout. It's miles from town and there's no chance they'll find us here. Best of all, the house is deserted.

Siddy   How d'you know it's deserted . . . I mean, real deserted?

Cobby   Well, look at it!

Siddy   You look. I think I'll keep me eyes closed and pretend I'm home in me own little bed.

Cobby   *(scornfully)* Siddy the Squizz, the fearless cat burglar, scared half to death by his own shadow! I tell you, there's been no-one here for years. Cobwebs, dust, bats — it's a real ghost house!

Siddy   *(horrified)* Don't say that, Cobby! Ghosts — blimey! I feel like someone is starin' at me — and enjoyin' it . . .

*(Behind them the closet door closes with a bang. **Siddy's** eyes bulge in terror.)*

What . . . was . . . that?

Cobby   The wind.

Siddy   It wasn't the wind that grabbed me out in the yard.

Cobby   That was the branches of that big elm tree. I told you not to walk under it.

Siddy It felt more like cold, clammy fingers clawin' at me throat!

Cobby Forget it and help me find a safe place to hide the diamonds. Got the torch?

(Siddy produces a torch from his coat pocket.)

Siddy Is it safe to turn it on?

Cobby Give over, Siddy, the police are miles away. Here, shine it on these little beauties.

*(He takes a necklace from his pocket. **Siddy** shines the torch on them.)*

The Van Heuson diamonds are now under new ownership!

Siddy Must be worth ten thousand, Cobby.

Cobby We're rich, Siddy, rich! We'll just lie low here for a few days then head for Europe.

Siddy *(quaking)* Here . . . for a few days . . . and nights?

Cobby Sure, Siddy. By that time they'll be looking fifty miles away and we'll be in the clear.

Siddy If I don't die of the horrors in the meantime.

Cobby   We'll hide the diamonds in this vase here.

(He drops the necklace in the vase.)

Now let's have a look round.

*(**Siddy** sweeps the beam to the left. It lights up the covered chair.)*

Siddy   *(terrified)* What's that?

Cobby   Just a chair covered with a sheet. Put the tools in it so we'll know where to find them.

*(**Siddy** crosses and dumps the bag in the chair. As he turns back, an arm comes out from beneath the sheet, gropes for the bag, picks it up and drops it on the floor with a clatter. The two men swing round.)*

Cobby   Thought I told you to put the bag in the chair.

Siddy   *(his voice shaking)* I thought I did. It must have . . . slipped off . . . I think . . .

Cobby   Leave it and come over here. There's a staircase to the upper floor.

*(**Siddy** shines the torch up the stairs.)*

Siddy   Are we goin' up?

Cobby   Later. Won't that raise your spirits?

Siddy   Stop it, Cobby — you just took ten years off me life!

(He swings the torch around and on to the statue.)

Aaaaaah!

Cobby   Quiet, Siddy, it's only a statue.

Siddy   Cor, it stood me hair clean off me head, it did.

(He goes over and pokes the statue with his finger.)

Statue   *(softly)* Ooooooh.

*(**Siddy** scuttles over to **Cobby**.)*

Siddy   Who said that?

Cobby   Just the wind again.

Siddy   It seemed to come from under that sheet. Cobby, there didn't feel to be anything under it . . . except air.

Cobby   Have a look then.

Siddy   Not me! I ain't stayin' here with spooks and empty statues! It ain't human!

*(He heads for the door. **Cobby** is amused.)*

Cobby   Look out for that elm tree. Come to think of it, I'm not sure it was a tree. That big knot did seem to be like a face, all twisted, with huge teeth . . .

*(**Siddy** changes direction and heads back for **Cobby**.)*

Siddy   I'm trapped! It's some awful nightmare and me mum's not here to wake me up!

*(**Cobby** crosses left to the big window and pulls the drapes across.)*

Cobby   No sense inviting trouble. Here Siddy, there's a sash hanging from the ceiling. In the old days they used to pull it to call the servants. *(He acts the part.)* Shall I order a glass of blood, my lord?

*(He tugs the sash and a deafening gong is heard. Instantly the lights come on and **Blud**, the butler, is standing at the head of the stairs. He is a tall, thin man, dressed in black tails and tie, all of which give the general impression of mustiness. His face is very white and his lips red but his expression never changes. **Siddy** freezes in terror and **Cobby's** hand flies to his pocket.)*

Blud   Good evening, gentlemen.

Siddy   Take him away! Take him away!

Cobby   *(in a tough voice)* All right, bud, who are you?

Blud   My name, sir, is Blud, not Bud. I am the butler.

*(He comes to the bottom of the stairs. **Siddy** backs up.)*

Cobby   Someone lives here?

Blud   Lord Reginald Freckleby, retired 1910, and Lady Freckleby.

Siddy   Retired 1910 . . . lor, he must be gettin' on by now.

Blud Indeed his lordship hardly shows his age. Remarkably well preserved.

*(**Cobby** comes across. **Siddy** cowers behind him.)*

Cobby We just ducked in out of the rain, sort of, thinking the place was deserted.

Blud Most of the year, Mudslow Manor *is* deserted, sir. His lordship's real home is Greenfriars.

Siddy *(whispering)* Cobby, that's a cemetery — nothin' there but tombstones!

Cobby Quiet, Siddy. Is his lordship home, then?

Blud Oh, yes sir — we're expecting several guests.

Siddy But it's gone midnight!

Blud His lordship believes that midnight is the best time for a little — spirited gathering.

Siddy *(backing away)* I knew it! I knew it! Ghosts, vampires —

Blud There has never been a vampire at Mudslow Manor, sir. And I've been butler here since 1890.

Siddy Cripes, how old are you?

Blud On these rainy nights, sir, I feel every bit of a hundred and fifty.

Siddy He looks it too, Cobby.

Blud If you will excuse me, I'll get his lordship.

(He disappears up the stairs.)

Siddy Now's our chance, Cobby. I'd rather have a tree chasin' me than him!

(Again he heads for the door.)

Cobby Siddy, don't you see the goldmine we've stumbled into? Think of the loot these rich people must have stashed away. All we have to do is get invited for the night.

Siddy I ain't stayin' the night with that Dracula wanderin' around!

(But he stops at the door.)

Cobby But it'll make the diamonds look like chicken feed. We'll clean up and retire for life.

Siddy Cor, I don't think I got much life left.

(He comes back.)

Oh, all right, Cobby — but I don't like it.

Cobby Good! Here's the plan. We'll wait until everyone has gone to bed, then we'll sneak down — sssh!

*(**Lord** and **Lady Reginald Freckleby** have appeared on the staircase. They are in formal dress, rather outdated and dusty perhaps, but really quite regal. **Lady Freckleby** glitters with diamonds. Preceded by **Blud**, they descend the staircase.)*

Cobby *(whispering)* Siddy, look at those diamonds.

Blud Lord and Lady Reginald Freckleby.

Lord Freckleby Good evening.

*(**Cobby** and **Siddy** take off their hats and bow deeply.)*

Cobby How d'you do, your lordship and ladyship.

Siddy How do, your highnesses.

Lady Freckleby Charmed, I'm sure.

Lord Freckleby I don't believe Blud gave us your names.

Cobby I'm Cobby, he's Siddy. We just came in to get out of the rain.

Siddy It ain't half horrible out there. Me boots is full of slosh.

Lady Freckleby Oh, really? I thought it was such splendid weather — or has it fined up? There's nothing like a good storm to get you in the mood.

Siddy *(quaking)* The mood for what?

Lady Freckleby Oh, just flitting around.

Lord Freckleby It's so very kind of you to call. We get so few callers.

Siddy *(looking around)* I can believe that.

Lord Freckleby Actually you were very lucky to find us in.

Siddy Luck, he calls it!

Lord Freckleby Yes, we came out here for a rest. Greenfriars isn't what it used to be you know. Can't get a wink of sleep there with all those new-fangled machines roaring up and down the road all day. Ah, give me the good old horse and carriage.

Cobby You like a good sleep then, do you your lordship?

Lord Freckleby *(peering at him closely)* Don't we all?

Siddy Cobby, do you know any good prayers?

Lady Freckleby You must do us the honour of staying the night.

Siddy Must we?

Cobby Thank you, your ladyship. I must say we could do with a cup of tea and a bowl of soup.

Blud I'm afraid, sir, that we have no food in the house.

Siddy No food? Blimey, how do you live then?

Lady Freckleby Live? I beg your pardon.

Blud I should point out, your ladyship, that Mr Cobby and Mr Siddy are from . . . out there.

Lady Freckleby Really? How interesting.

*(**Siddy** has his eyes tightly closed.)*

Siddy Our Father, who art in heaven—

Lord Freckleby Of course, we're expecting other guests during the evening.

Blud I have reason to believe that several have already arrived, m'lord.

Lord Freckleby Then they're probably drying out somewhere or having a snooze in the basement. We won't disturb them.

Cobby We didn't see any.

Lord Freckleby You wouldn't. They turn up in the oddest places.

Siddy *(still praying)* I'll lift me eyes up to the hills from whence cometh me help . . .

(He continues silently.)

Cobby *(whispering)* Siddy, you'll blow the whole game!

*(The outer door bursts open and **Priscilla**, a young girl of about fourteen, runs in. She is dressed in a long white frock which looks suspiciously like a draped sheet. In her hand she carries a shovel.)*

Priscilla *(stopping short)* Oh, hullo.

Lord Freckleby Our niece, Priscilla. Priscilla, this is Mr Cobby and Mr Siddy who are spending the night with us.

Cobby Pleased to meet you, Miss.

*(**Siddy** is only just opening his eyes again.)*

Lady Freckleby Priscilla, where in earth have you been?

Priscilla Just putting Coffin to bed, Auntie.

Siddy With a shovel?

Blud Coffin is the family dog, sir.

Siddy Oh, that explains it . . . no, it doesn't!

Priscilla His poor little leg still troubles him, Uncle.

Lord Freckleby Never mind, dear, it's probably the wet ground.

Priscilla Can I bring him indoors tomorrow?

Lord Freckleby Of course. Blud will dig a bed for him in the basement.

Priscilla Oh, goody! Right next to mine!

Siddy *(horrified)* You mean . . . ? Cobby, I don't think I'm scared any more. I think I'm going crazy.

Cobby Ssssh, Siddy — it's all an act.

Lady Freckleby Now, Priscilla, go upstairs and clean up before our guests arrive. You'll find a fresh sheet in the cupboard. Blud, show our friends to the spare room in the west wing. The black room, I think — black is such a restful colour.

Blud Yes, m'lady.

Lady Freckleby Everything is prepared. Priscilla dusted off the slabs this morning. Or would you prefer a box? Far more private but a little too cramped, I always think.

Cobby No, no — a slab will do fine.

Lady Freckleby Splendid. We'll bid you a very good evening then. Please excuse any other guests you may see . . . hanging around.

Siddy We'll keep our door locked.

Lady Freckleby That hardly matters, does it?

Cobby *(quickly)* They won't disturb us. We sleep like the dead.

Lady Freckleby Really? How interesting.

> *(**Lord** and **Lady Freckleby** disappear up the stairs. **Priscilla** takes the shovel and leans it against the wall, right. **Blud** moves round behind **Cobby** and **Siddy**.)*

Priscilla I'll leave the shovel here, Blud, just in case you run out of beds when the guests arrive.

Blud Very good, Miss Priscilla.

> *(**Priscilla** goes up the stairs.)*

Cobby How did your dog hurt his leg, Priscilla?

Priscilla *(turning)* He was run over by a butcher's cart.

Siddy Was he hurt bad?

Priscilla No. He was killed. Night.

*(She disappears up the stairs. **Siddy** turns and heads for the door but runs into **Blud** and almost faints.)*

Blud This way, gentlemen.

(He holds them, one in each huge hand, and steers them up the stairs.)

Blud Your room is very comfortable. I'm sure you'll . . . rest in peace.

Siddy Ooooooooh!

*(Without changing his expression **Blud** gives a long, maniacal laugh and half drags them up the stairs. The lights dim and all is quiet, deathly quiet. Suddenly something taps on the curtained window pane. The covered statue starts, stretches wide its 'arms' and yawns loudly. Then it turns round revealing two small eye holes and the end of an arrow sticking out of the sheet where the chest should be. It moves across to the banister and scratches its back against it, sighing in contentment. Another tap is heard at the window. The statue glides across, draws back the curtains and opens the window.)*

Hood Hulloooooooooooooooo —

*(The closet door opens and the skeleton steps out. It has a three-cornered Napoleonic hat on its head and a sword and bugle at its waist. It creeps over behind **Hood** and raises its arms menacingly.)*

Napoleon Boo!

Hood Aaaah!

*(**Hood** jumps in fright and spins round.)*

Did you have to do that? I'm still waking up.

Napoleon Sorry, but I have to keep in practice. Do you always sleep standing up?

Hood Ever tried to lie down with an arrow sticking out of your ribs?

Napoleon *(looking down at himself ruefully)* It wouldn't worry me.

Hood Who are you?

Napoleon I'm all that's left of poor Napoleon Bonaparte. Get it? Bone apart.

Hood Very funny. Ha, ha!

Napoleon Please don't make me laugh. I'm getting rather loose these days. One good laugh and I'll fall apart, just like a jigsaw puzzle.

Hood Sorry. How did you get into that closet? When I tried the door it was locked.

Napoleon I used a skeleton key.

Hood Of course. Ha, ha — oops, there I go again.

Napoleon That's all right. Most of the time I manage to keep a straight face — and with me that's not very hard.

(They move to the centre of the room.)

That's a funny place to wear an arrow.

Hood I'm Robin Hood. I was doing all right in Sherwood Forest, robbing the rich and giving it all to the poor —

Napoleon That's a silly idea.

Hood Why? I was pretty poor myself.

Napoleon That's a good idea. I always say the only good thief is a heartless thief — like me.

Hood Ha, ha — oh, dear. Anyway, one day Friar Tuck told me I was such a bad shot I couldn't hit myself. I wasn't and I did.
I shot an arrow into the air,
It fell to earth and struck me there.

Napoleon By the way, have you seen Dr Stein? He was right here when I ducked into the closet to polish my skull.

Hood Do you mean the gentleman in the chair?

*(**Napoleon** goes over and peers under the sheet.)*

Napoleon Dr Stein?

*(**Stein** comes out from under the sheet. He is a small man, shabbily dressed in nineteenth-century clothes. He has a beard and rimless glasses set on a very white face.)*

Stein *(stretching)* Evening Bones. Just having a doze.

Napoleon Meet Robin Hood. Robin, this is Dr Frank N. Stein.

*(**Stein** shakes the 'hand' offered by **Hood**.)*

Hood Aren't you the famous health expert who advertises body-building courses in the 'Ghostly Gazette'?

Stein The same.

Napoleon Never helped me. *(He sighs.)* Too far gone.

Hood And wasn't it you who made that awful monster?

Stein Alas — yes, the horrible brute. It's outside now pretending to be an elm tree. It's all green. That's why it's pretending to be a tree.

Hood Why did you make it green?

Stein Actually I started out to build a nice pine for my front garden, then my plans got mixed up. By the time I realized my mistake I was up there on the ladder screwing its ears on.

Hood What a frightening experience!

Stein I'll say! I screwed its ears on back to front and it's never forgiven me. It's been following me for a hundred years. I don't suppose either of you could use a good monster?

Napoleon Not me. Could have been a great help at Waterloo, though.

Hood Me neither. I don't have to worry about the Sheriff of Nottingham any more. *(He points to the floor.)* He's down there.

Stein Pity. Anyway, Bones, what are you doing in England?

Napoleon Oh, I came over for my annual reunion with Nelson and Wellington. Splendid chap, Nelson, once you get him down off that dirty great column. And as for Wellington — well, I've long since let bygones be bygones.

Stein I must say you don't look well. Lost a bit of weight, have you?

Napoleon A bit! No wonder I'm so thin — I can't eat anything! It falls straight out on the floor! For a while I used to be just skin and bone — now I'm not even that.

Hood Cheer up. In another two hundred years you'll be just like me.

Napoleon But what'll I do till then? None of the girls will speak to me. I met that beautiful Joan of Arc at the Spirits Barbecue last week and she got all burned up over nothing. I showed her my medals but she looked straight through me and went off to share a steak with Ivan the Terrible. And Florence Nightingale wouldn't have anything to do with a nobody running around without any clothes on.

Hood You certainly are straight up and down.

Stein Everyone has troubles. I've got a monster of a headache and can't get rid of it.

Hood And I've got to wear this arrow for the rest of my days — which is forever. Awfully difficult when I ask a girl to dance to one of those haunting melodies.

Stein Oh come on, cheer up everyone. We shouldn't look so grave on such a beautiful evening. What we need is a good haunt to buck us up!

Hood What about those bounders who were in here earlier?

Napoleon   The cads! I've got a bone to pick with those two.

Stein   Did you see them hide something?

Hood   Yes, in that vase.

(He goes over and takes the diamonds from the vase.)

Napoleon   Are they real?

Stein   Of course they are — diamonds don't have ghosts.

*(**Hood** holds the diamonds against his chest.)*

Hood   They look smashing against my hood. Set off the arrow, don't you think?

Napoleon   Who said they were yours?

Hood   I did. Any objections, skinny?

Napoleon   Plenty. Dr Stein thought of them first.

Hood   How would you like to be haunted by a flying arrow for the rest of eternity?

Napoleon   Huh! Just like Nelson and Wellington — thieve anything they can get their hands on!

*(They face up to each other but **Stein** intervenes.)*

Stein   Gentlemen, gentlemen! Remember our first job is to stop these criminals from robbing our dear hosts.

Hood   Sorry.

(He drops the diamonds onto the table.)

Napoleon   Me too. I'll phone Sherlock Holmes at Scotland Yard. I've got a ghost line in my closet.

Hood   And we'll teach them a jolly good lesson, too. Let's give them a first-degree haunting!

Stein   Why not make it a contest? Whoever haunts them the best gets the diamonds.

Napoleon   Good show! Who goes first?

Hood   Not me. They might have guns.

Stein   Why worry? The bullets'll go straight through you.

Hood   I know. But they tickle —

Stein   I can hear them coming, so we'd better get ready. Robin, put the diamonds back in the vase. (*Hood does so.*) Now I'll go first, then Robin, then Bones. To your places, gentlemen!

(*Hood goes back to his position as a statue. Stein gets under the sheet in the chair and Napoleon smoothes it over him. Then he disappears into the closet. The lights come up slightly and after a moment Cobby and Siddy creep cautiously down the stairs and into the room.*)

Siddy   Do you think they're asleep, Cobby?

Cobby   Dead to the world. (*Siddy groans.*) I'll get the diamonds and you have a look round and see if you can spot the safe.

Siddy   All right — but I don't like it, Cobby.

(*Cobby gets the diamonds and stands admiring them. Siddy begins to look under the pictures on the wall, left. Hood moans loudly and the closet door opens slightly.*)

Napoleon   (*in a loud whisper*) Wait your turn, Hood!

(*The closet door slams shut. Siddy is paralysed with terror and Cobby looks around, startled, and drops the diamonds onto the table.*)

Siddy   That does it! I'm gettin' me tools and goin'!

(*He goes over to the covered chair. As he does so he treads on the edge of the sheet. There is a loud cry of pain.*)

Stein   Would you mind getting off my toe?

(*Siddy, his eyes bulging, runs over behind Cobby, who draws a revolver from his pocket.*)

Siddy   There's . . . someone . . . under it, Cobby.

(*Cobby walks over and pulls off the sheet.*)

Stein   Good evening.

Siddy   Oh my gawd, it's a spook, a real spook!

Cobby   Nah — it's some old loon dressed up.

Stein   *(standing)* Dr Frank N. Stein at your service.

Siddy   I knew it — Frankenstein!

Cobby   You don't fool me, Stein! What's your game?

Stein   My game, sir, is selling used monsters. Would you happen to require one in excellent working order? I could arrange a little demonstration —

Cobby   A monster? You don't scare us, Stein.

Siddy   Yes he does, yes he does!

Stein   Really?

(He goes to the window and calls out.)

Hey, you — monster! Are you still out there? You with the funny ears!

*(There is a mighty roar of anger and a hideous green hand reaches in the window and claws the air. Then it withdraws. **Siddy** nearly faints from terror. **Cobby** is profoundly shaken but still game.)*

Siddy   Make a run for it, Cobby! Anything but this!

Cobby   He's on to us, Siddy! He's got a mate outside and they're after our diamonds!

Stein   Shall I call him in, then?

Siddy   No, no!

Cobby   You won't get away with it, Stein!

*(There is a loud moan from **Hood**. Neither **Cobby** nor **Siddy** looks around.)*

And you can tell your friend to stop making the funny noises.

*(Unseen, **Hood** glides over and stands behind **Siddy**. Then he utters a horrible moan and wraps his arms around **Siddy's** neck.)*

Siddy   Cobby, help me! One of them's got me!

*(**Cobby** levels his gun at **Hood**.)*

Cobby   Let him go or I'll shoot!

*(**Hood** lets **Siddy** go and he slumps to the floor, covering his face with his hands. **Hood** flaps his hands above his head.)*

Hood   Boooooooooo!

Cobby   You asked for it!

*(He fires once at **Hood**, who drops his arms and giggles loudly.)*

Hood   Ooooooh — that tickles!

Cobby   I'm seeing things! It went straight through him!

Siddy   We're gone, Cobby, finished!

Cobby   Not yet we aren't!

*(He dashes for the diamonds. Suddenly the closet door bursts open and **Napoleon** charges into the room, brandishing sword and bugle.)*

Napoleon   Down with the English! Man the guns! Blow them apart, boys! Vive la France!

*(He blows a long blast on his bugle. **Siddy** faints and lies flat on his back. **Cobby** backs away, waving his gun in front of him.)*

Cobby   Keep away! Don't touch me!

*(He backs into **Stein**.)*

Stein   A jolly good boo to you, sir!

*(**Cobby** spins away and backs to the window. **Hood** flaps his arms and **Napoleon** advances.)*

Hood   Booooooooooo!

Napoleon   Level the forty-pounders at his head, gunner!

Cobby   Go away! Go away!

*(**Cobby** slams against the window. There is a roar from outside and the green arm comes through and wraps itself around **Cobby's** throat. He squirms round and stares out.)*

The tree! It's alive! Aaaaaaaaah —

(He faints and slumps down against the wall. The arm, after a couble

more swipes, disappears. **Hood**, **Stein** *and* **Napoleon** *gather in the centre of the room.)*

Stein   And that, gentlemen, is that! A deadly haunting, even if I say so myself.

Hood   You mean they've joined us?

Stein   Not quite — just fainted.

Hood   Pity. I could have used them amongst my merry ghosts.

*(**Napoleon** has placed the diamonds around his neck.)*

Napoleon   Well, I believe I've earned these.

Hood   Just a minute, you miserable stack of bones — it was the monster who did the trick!

Napoleon   Keep off or I'll pull out your arrow and let you down like a big fat balloon!

(There is a loud knock at the door.)

Stein   Ssssh — I'll see who it is.

(He goes to the window.)

Police! Did you ring Sherlock Holmes, Bones?

Napoleon   Yes.

Stein   This is the real police. We'd better hide.

*(They resume their former positions. The door is banged loudly again. The lights come fully up as **Blud** comes down the stairs, crosses the room and opens the door.)*

Blud   Good evening, may I help you?

*(**Inspector Hoam** and **Sergeant Watkins** come just inside the door, staring open-mouthed at **Blud**.)*

Hoam   I'm . . . I'm Inspector Hoam and this is Sergeant Watkins. We're from the local police . . .

*(**Lord** and **Lady Freckleby** have appeared on the stairs and, between them, **Priscilla**.)*

Lord Freckleby   Who is it, Blud?

Blud The police, m'lord — the *real* police.

Hoam Hoam is the name, sir, Hoam and Watkins.

Lord Freckleby Do come in.

> *(The police walk into the room.* **Lord** *and* **Lady Freckleby** *descend the stairs.* **Priscilla** *goes over to* **Siddy**.*)*

Watkins These look like our birds, Inspector.

> *(He points at* **Siddy** *and* **Cobby**.*)*

Hoam A message was relayed from Scotland Yard saying these men were seen near here. They received a call from some crackpot asking for Sherlock Holmes. Said he was Napoleon.

Lady Freckleby Indeed. Are they criminals, Inspector?

Hoam A desperate pair of ruffians, m'm, wanted for robbery. Seems we've come too late.

> *(***Watkins*** *examines* **Siddy**.*)*

Watkins They're not dead — just fainted, sir. Looks like he's scared stiff.

Hoam Cobby and Con and Siddy the Squizz, two of our toughest crooks! What happened?

Blud I believe the storm frightened them, sir.

Watkins Inspector, Siddy's coming around.

> *(***Siddy*** *sits up, staring at* **Watkins**.*)*

Siddy Another one! Another one!

Watkins Calm down, Siddy — you know me.

Siddy *(clutching him)* Thank heavens — the police!

Watkins Steady on there!

Siddy Don't let them get me!

Hoam *(coming over)* Don't let who get you?

Siddy Ghosts, skeletons, monsters! The house is overrun with them! There! *(He points at the statue.)*

Hoam   Check that, Watkins. (**Watkins** *goes over and prods the statue.*)

Watkins   Just a sheet hanging on a wire.

Blud   It used to cover the grand piano, sir.

Siddy   In the chair, then!

(**Watkins** *looks under the sheet on the chair.*)

Watkins   A pile of old rags, nothing else.

Hoam   All right, Siddy, you're not talking your way out of this one.

Siddy   (*frantic*) I'm telling the truth! There's a skeleton in the closet!

(**Watkins** *goes over and opens the closet door.*)

Watkins   Only a broom. And look what we have here.

(*He lifts out the broom. It has* **Napoleon's** *hat on it — and the diamonds.*)

Hoam   Slipped that time, Siddy. Led us right to the diamonds.

(**Watkins** *takes the diamonds, returns the broom and shuts the door.* **Siddy** *moans.* **Blud** *leans over him.*)

Blud   Would the gentleman like a nice glass of water?

Siddy   (*clutching at* **Hoam**) Keep him away! Keep them all away! Lock me up and throw away the key!

Hoam   We'll do just that, Siddy my boy. Get hold of Cobby, Watkins.

(**Watkins** *lifts* **Cobby** *to his feet.* **Priscilla** *leans over* **Siddy**.)

Priscilla   Coffin and I will visit you every night, Mr Siddy.

Siddy   No . . . no . . . (*He faints again.*)

Hoam   There'll be a reward, sir. This house is your permanent address, I take it?

Lord Freckleby   Oh no — you can reach us at Greenfriars.

Watkins   (*alarmed*) That's a cemetery, sir.

Hoam   And your names?

Lord Freckleby   Lord and Lady Reginald Freckleby.

Watkins *(shaking)* Sir, Lord and Lady Freckleby of Mudslow Manor died fifty years ago. They and their niece were killed when their carriage plunged over a cliff . . .

Hoam *(nervous)* Then these people must be . . . who did they say rang the Yard, Watkins?

Watkins Napoleon, he said.

Lord Freckleby Oh, that's only Bones — a friend of ours.

Hoam Why . . . do you . . . call him . . . Bones?

(A loud laugh comes from the closet.)

Watkins What was that?

Blud The radio, sir.

Watkins At this hour? And in the closet?

Hoam Come on, Watkins, let's get out of here!

Watkins Coming at the run, sir!

(They hurry out with **Cobby** *and* **Siddy**. **Blud** *crosses and shuts the door behind them.)*

Lord Freckleby   Well I never! I could have sworn those two young men were honest. They might have burgled us of all our possessions.

Lady Freckleby   And we have our guests to thank for saving us. I believe they can come out of hiding now.

*(***Blud*** *takes the cover off* **Stein**. **Hood** *turns round and stretches.)*

Lord Freckleby   Gentlemen, we are indeed grateful.

Stein   Tut, it was nothing. A most enjoyable haunt.

Priscilla   Where's Napoleon?

Stein   Still in the closet.

(He goes over to the closet and opens it.)

Oh, no!

Hood   What is it?

*(***Stein*** *holds up a big white bone.)*

Stein   Just a heap of bones!

Hood   He shouldn't have laughed so hard.

Priscilla   Poor Napoleon, he'll have to spend the rest of eternity in a box.

Lord Freckleby   Dr Stein, do you think you could put him back together again with wire and glue?

Stein   Of course. I'm sure I can do a perfect job — but I hope he won't mind if I screw his ears on back to front —

(As if in answer, there comes a yell from the closet followed by a roar from outside and the green arm reaches through the window and shakes its fist at **Stein**.)

By the way, Lord Freckleby, could I interest you in one slightly used monster?

CURTAIN

Questions

1 How did Lord and Lady Freckleby and their niece, Priscilla, die?

2 What is the first real indication we have that the house *is* haunted?

3 Which of the two robbers is the 'tougher'? Give reasons for your answer.

4 Explain why, when Siddy enquires how they live, Lady Freckleby asks: 'Live? I beg your pardon.'

5 'I met that beautiful Joan of Arc at the Spirits Barbecue last week and she got all burned up over nothing.' What particular humorous technique is being used here? Explain how it achieves its effect.

6 Why would Napoleon have had to 'let bygones be bygones' in order to associate with Wellington?

7 Explain why Hood's idea of robbing the rich and giving to the poor at first seems silly to Napoleon. Why does he change his mind and decide that it is not so silly after all?

8 Why does Hood not want to be shot?

9 Account for Watkins's surprise when Lord Freckleby says they can be reached at Greenfriars.

10 Explain why all Watkins finds in the closet is a broom with Napoleon's hat on it. What has happened to his bones, and why did it happen?

Richard Tydeman

```
                        Cast
Narrator
Fanny Adams ........................ Sweet seventeen
Grandmother ........................ Sweet seventy-seven
Percival ................................ Young and handsome
Sir Jasper ............................ Dark and villainous
Ma Adams ............................ Fanny's mother
Pa Adams ............................ Fanny's father
A Princess
First Village Girl
Second Village Girl
Third Village Girl
Fourth Village Girl
```

SCENE I

The Village Green. (One seat required.)

*(The **Narrator** appears before the curtain, book in hand.)*

Narrator   If you have tears, prepare to let them flow;
My tale is one of tragedy and woe . . .
A tale to set your fluttering heart a-quiver,
And stir your vitals to the very liver.
So, ladies and gentlemen, I pray you heed,
While my sad tale I tell — or rather read . . .
(For let me now admit, before we start:
I haven't had the time to learn me part!)
But first, let's look upon a merry scene:
Sweet maidens dancing on the village green.

*(Curtain up. **Narrator** moves to side of stage. **Girls** are dancing. Opportunity for maypole dance, country dance, chorus, etc. If preferred, **Girls** could just dance a few steps and then go straight on with the action.)*

What grace! What beauty! What a charming sight!
But who is this with sparkling eyes so bright,

*(Enter **Fanny**, supporting her aged **Grandmother**.)*

Supporting on one arm her ancient Granny?
What is your name, sweet maid?

Fanny   *(with a curtsey)*   My name is Fanny.

1st Girl   'Tis Fanny, seventeen years old today.
Let's wish her joy to cheer her on her way.

*(**Girls** dance round; or they could sing 'Happy Birthday to you . . .' etc.)*

Narrator   Sweet Fanny's shy, as modest maidens are;
But with a blush she softly answers:

Fanny   Ta.

*(**Fanny** buries her face in **Granny's** shoulder. Enter **Percival**.)*

Narrator   But who is this blue-eyed, well-favoured youth,
His face aglow with honesty and truth,
As strong as Samson and as proud as Nero?
It is, of course, young Percival, our hero.

Percival Miss Fanny, I ... I, I ... Miss Fanny, I, I, I ...
Miss Fanny, I ...

Narrator *(to Chorus of **Girls**)* Ay, ay?

Girls   Ay, ay!

*(With nods and winks of understanding, the **Girls** go off.)*

Narrator Now Granny sits, pretending not to see,
As Percival goes down upon his knee:

Percival Miss Fanny, I — if I may dare address you ...
I wish — I wish — I wish ...

Granny *(sneezing)* A-tishoo!

Percival   Bless you.

Fanny Dear Granny, are you ill?

Granny   No, no, my dear,
'tis just a cold. I must go in, I fear.

Fanny Yes, yes. *(To **Percival**.)* Oh Sir, what you are trying to say,
I'll gladly listen to, another day.

Percival *(bowing awkwardly)* Your servant, ladies. From my very heart,
I bid — I say — I wish — I — I'll depart. *(Goes out.)*

Narrator The ladies start their footsteps to retrace,
When suddenly before them, face to face,

*(Enter **Sir Jasper**.)*

There stands a figure threatening and tall:
It is the young Sir Jasper from The Hall.

Sir Jasper Aha, what have we here? Two ladies fair?
Allow me to escort you.

Fanny Sir, forbear!
My Granny's ill.

Narrator The words are scarcely spoken,
When like a tree by gales and tempest broken,
Poor Granny sways, and swinging slowly round,
Clutching the air, falls fainting to the ground.

*(**Granny** does a spectacular and impressive faint.)*

Fanny cries out:

Fanny Oh, fetch some water, Hurry!

Narrator But bad Sir Jasper doesn't seem to worry.
In fact he finds this chance too good to miss;
While Granny's out, he tries to steal a kiss.
But Fanny quickly puts him in his place,
And while he smacks his lips, she smacks his face.
Her cries are heard in time of greatest need,
As Percival returns at break-neck speed.

*(**Percival** runs in, out of breath.)*

He's nearly rendered speechless by the view:

Percival Eh? Eh? *(Pronounced 'A, A.')*

*(Seeing **Granny**.)* Ee! Ee!
*(Turning to **Fanny**.)* I — I . . .
*(As **Fanny** points to **Sir Jasper**.)* Oh! Oh!
*(Going up to **Sir Jasper** threateningly.)* You, you . . . !

Narrator   Come, gentlemen, there is no time to fight.
        We must get poor old Granny home tonight.

*(**Percival** and **Sir Jasper** raise **Granny** to her feet. Each takes one arm and they start off in opposite directions. **Granny** is pulled from side to side, with **Fanny** anxiously clasping her hands and running to and fro with them.)*

Narrator   Stop, stop at once! That's not the way to shift her.
        The stronger of the two of you must lift her.

Sir Jasper   That's I! *(He tries to lift **Granny**.)*

Percival   That's me! *(He pushes **Sir Jasper** away.)*

Sir Jasper   That's I!

Percival   I'll see you boiled!

*(**Percival** scoops up **Granny** in his arms.)*

Sir Jasper   Then I'll have this one!

*(He tries to catch **Fanny**, who runs from him and darts behind **Percival**. As **Sir Jasper** runs towards them, **Percival** thrusts **Granny** into his arms, scoops up **Fanny** and goes out. **Sir Jasper**, still holding **Granny**, turns towards the audience:)*

Foiled!

*(Curtain falls, leaving **Narrator** outside.)*

SCENE II

Fanny's cottage. (Three chairs and a table required.)

Narrator   Time flies; and when we reach the second scene,
        Twelve months have passed, and Fanny's now eighteen.
        Sir Jasper's father, the old Squire, is dead,
        And so Sir Jasper's now the Squire instead.
        His cruel deeds, his villainy and pride,
        Are soon the talk of all the countryside.
        Only two people have not heard the truth,
        And still regard him as a virtuous youth;
        And in their humble cottage here they are:
        The Adamses, our Fanny's Ma and Pa.

*(Curtain rises, revealing **Ma** and **Pa**, seated perfectly still, with blank expressions on their faces as if posing for a passport photograph.)*

Behold their faces, bland and innocent,
When Squire Jasper calls to take the rent.

*(There is a knock at the door. **Ma** gets up. **Pa** gently makes her sit down again, goes to door and opens it, stepping back with a smile and a bow. **Ma** rises and curtseys. Enter **Sir Jasper**. They get him the best chair and he sits, patronisingly waving them to be seated, too. They sit on the edge of their chairs. **Sir Jasper** gives **Pa** a cigar which he receives with incredulity and delight, and places reverently in his top pocket.)*

The Squire speaks, as mild as milk and water:

Sir Jasper   Now tell me, pray, where is your charming daughter?

*(**Ma** goes off to fetch **Fanny**.)*

Pa Adams   She's gone upstairs, her Granny's fire to tend.
Alas, poor Granny's very near her end.

Narrator   This gives the Squire another bright idea.
He beckons Pa, and whispers in his ear.
What is he saying? Pa seems quite excited,
And clasps the Squire's hand as if delighted.

*(Re-enter **Ma** with **Fanny**.)*

The Squire speaks:

Sir Jasper   Miss Fanny, how'd it be
If I take Granny to The Hall with me?

Narrator   On hearing this, poor Fanny gives a start.

Fanny   I love my Granny. We shall never part.

Narrator   Of course that's what the villain hoped she'd say.

Sir Jasper   Then you may come as well. We'll start today.

Narrator   At this, the damsel shrinks back in alarm;
But Ma and Pa each take her by the arm:

Pa Adams   Come now, Fanny, no one's going to bite you.

Ma Adams   'Tis very kind of Squire to invite you.

Pa Adams   For Granny's sake, you must go with her, Fan.

Ma Adams   Squire's such a pleasant, well-behaved young man.

Narrator   The maiden shrieks and runs upstairs in grief.

(*Fanny* goes out.)

While Pa and Ma just stare in unbelief.
The Squire hides a scowl behind his hand,
Then turns and speaks in accents calm and bland:

Sir Jasper   I hope you'll help Miss Fanny change her mind.

Ma Adams   Oh Squire, Sir Jasper, you are more than kind.
I'll see she comes; and so will father, too.

Pa Adams   (*doubtfully*) Yet she's entitled to her point of view.

Narrator   It's plain to see that Pa is sunk in doubt;
But quickly Squire contrives to pull him out:
Dissembling his devilish intent,
Says casually:

Sir Jasper   Oh, about the rent . . .

Pa Adams   Forgive me, Squire, I'll go at once and get it.

Sir Jasper No, no, just for this week we will forget it.

Narrator The dear good man can scarce believe his ears;
But when he understands, his doubts and fears
Are swept away like ripples on the sea,
By such amazing generosity.
His honest face is shining like the moon.

Pa Adams Fanny and Gran shall come this afternoon.

Narrator Sir Jasper's eyes his triumph now betray,

(**Sir Jasper** *leers at the audience*.)

But hardly has the old man given way,
When Fanny enters, white as any ghost,

(*Re-enter* **Fanny**.)

And once more beats Sir Jasper at the post.

Fanny Poor Granny's sickness won't need me to nurse it.
Poor Granny's dead.

Ma Adams   Oh no!

Pa Adams   Oh bother!

Sir Jasper   Curse it!

Narrator He's foiled, but he recovers in a flash;
At least he'll rescue something from the crash.
And turning with a smile malevolent:

Sir Jasper Now, Adams, if you please, I'll have the rent!

(*Curtain falls leaving* **Narrator** *outside*.)

SCENE III

The Village Green.

Narrator As time goes on, things go from bad to worse;
(And so, I fear, does this atrocious verse:)
Her granny dead, her mother sick with care,
Poor Fanny's lot is hard indeed to bear;
For Squire Jasper woos with such insistence,

She has a job to make him keep his distance.
And where, you ask, is Percy all this time?
Alas, he's far away in foreign clime;
The crafty Squire secured him quick promotion
With shipping on the South Pacific Ocean.
And now it is the merry month of May,
When once again the maidens are at play.

(Curtain up. **Girls** *dancing, etc.)*

2nd Girl   What ever is poor Fanny going to do?
I'm glad I'm not her family, aren't you?

3rd Girl   Unless she says she'll marry Squire today,
He's going to turn them out of doors — they say.

4th Girl   I don't know why that causes Fanny sorrow;
If he asked me, I'd marry Squire tomorrow.

1st Girl   But then, he hasn't asked you, has he, dear?

2nd Girl   And isn't likely to, while Fanny's near.

Narrator   Now ladies, please: Meg, Mary, Jane, Georgina . . .
Here's Fanny now. Pretend you have not seen her.

(Girls dance on. Enter **Fanny***, slowly and sadly.)*

3rd Girl   Come dearest Fanny, why this downward glance?

4th Girl   Will you not join us in a merry dance?

Narrator   But Fanny sadly smiles and shakes her head.
The maidens dance off by themselves instead.

(Dance, and exeunt **Girls***.)*

Fanny soliloquises in this strain:

Fanny   If only Percival were home again,
Then would my troubles cease.

(Enter **Sir Jasper** *behind her.)*

Narrator   She gives a sigh.

Sir Jasper   Miss Fanny.

Fanny   Percy! *(Turning.)* Oh, it's you.

Sir Jasper   'Tis I.
    Proud maiden, marry me you surely shall.

Fanny   No no, my heart belongs to Percival.

Narrator   The cruel monster will not be denied;
    By hook or crook he'll have her for his bride.
    So, having failed again to plead his cause,
    A trump card from his pocket now he draws:
    A package, bearing on the title page,
    In blackest type the dreadful word 'MORTGAGE'.
    Fanny turns pale, for as she clearly knows,
    Sir Jasper has the power to foreclose;
    And if he does, why then without a doubt
    The Adamses will find themselves kicked out.
    The Squire turns on his heel, poor Fanny scorning,
    And barks:

Sir Jasper   I'll give you till tomorrow morning. *(Goes out.)*

Narrator   Now is the hour of Fanny's deepest woe.

Fanny   Oh Percival,

Narrator   She cries,

Fanny   I need you so!

Narrator   But though from hill to hill the echoes run,
          Yet, sad to tell you, answer came there none.
          For human voices, even when terrific,
          Can scarcely carry to the South Pacific.
          Let's leave the maiden in her dismal plight,
          And draw the curtain of sepulchral night.

*(Curtain falls, leaving **Narrator** outside.)*

SCENE IV

Fanny's cottage.

Narrator   We come now to our final scene, next day.
          The darkness of the night has passed away,
          The sun is shining at its fullest wattage,
          And we are once again at Fanny's cottage.

*(Curtain up. **Fanny** alone.)*

          Alas, although the day is bright and fair,
          Yet here is only gloom and black despair.
          Her father's gone to see his bank again,
          To ask how much his overdraft they'll strain.
          She sighs:

Fanny   Ah-ah!

Narrator   Which shows she's anxious, rather:
          And softly cries:

Fanny   What can be keeping father?

*(Enter **Pa Adams**.)*

Narrator   Her father now appears. She runs to meet him,
          And throws her arms around his neck to greet him.
          The old man's face is set as hard as flint;
          With tragic voice he croaks:

Pa Adams   My child, we're skint.

Narrator   By this he means he hasn't any money.

Pa Adams   Oh you may laugh, but this is far from funny.

Narrator   She leads him to a chair and strokes his brow.

Fanny   Dear father. Still, at least we have the cow.

Narrator   The old man very sadly shakes his head.

Pa Adams   Alas, my darling child, the cow is dead.

Narrator   Poor Fanny at this news is in despair;
She falls upon her knees and tears her hair.

   *(Enter **Ma Adams**.)*

Her mother now appears, thin, weak and ailing,
And when she hears the news, joins in the wailing.
Old man and daughter both cry even harder
When mother says:

Ma Adams   There's nothing in the larder.

Narrator   All three of them by now are weeping sore,
When suddenly a knock sounds at the door.
They huddle, frightened by the dreadful din,
And Mr Adams feebly calls:

Pa Adams   Come in.

   *(Enter **Sir Jasper**.)*

Narrator   The Squire appears from silver-plated car;
He curls his black moustache and cries:

Sir Jasper   Aha!

Narrator   The mortgage on the table now he throws.
No words are spoken. Everybody knows
Exactly what he means, as, head held high,
With folded arms he waits for his reply.
Now Fanny looks at Pa and Ma askance;
Reproachfully they both return her glance.
Her face poor Fanny vainly tries to hide;
When suddenly a noise is heard outside:

The sound of footsteps, followed by a knock,
The door swings back — prepare now for a shock!
You'd never guess it in a thousand years,
But in the doorway, Percival appears!

*(Enter **Percival**.)*

They stare, as if a ghost had come to call,
Till Percy brightly cries:

Percival   Good morning all.

Narrator   They all express their inmost feelings:

Ma Adams   Mercy!

Pa Adams   Well, blow me down!

Sir Jasper   Ten thousand curses!

Fanny   Percy!

Narrator   The damsel throws herself into his arms.
But this is not the end of their alarms;
For Percival, before you can say knife,
Goes on:

Percival   Please let me introduce — my wife.

Narrator   They're all struck dumb, as through the open door
They see a sight they've never seen before:
Her curly hair as black as any Zulu . . .
For Percy's wife has come from Honolulu.

*(Enter the **Princess**, **Percy's** wife, a native girl from the South Sea Islands. The **Girls** follow her in, staring.)*

Percival   My friends, meet Princess Lickee Cookee-pot.
Her father owns five gold-mines and a yacht.

Narrator   The Princess grins in manner truly frightful,
And says:

Princess   To meet you I am most delightful.

Narrator   Now Percy's rich, he throws his weight about.

Percival   *(picking up the mortage and looking at it)* How much? Two
hundred?

(Producing a handful of notes from his pocket.)
                                        Take it.

*(Thrusting notes at **Sir Jasper**.)*   Now, get out.

Narrator   The beaten Squire knows not which way to go.
But Fanny cannot bear to see him so.
For though it's true that beggars can't be choosers,
Her sympathy is always with the losers.

Pa Adams   We're saved! I've got my house.

Ma Adams   And I've got you.

Percival   I've got a wife, and all her money, too.

Sir Jasper   And I?

Pa Adams   You? You've got nothing.

Narrator   Steady, Daddums.
I rather think he gets Sweet Fanny Adams.

*(**Fanny** runs to **Sir Jasper** and embraces him.)*

(*Tableau.*)

The moral of this tale is plain to see:
If you desire a woman's sympathy,
Don't try to win, or she will just ignore you.
Be on the losing side, and she'll adore you.
May all your troubles thus be put to right.
And now, in unison we'll say:

All   Good night.

CURTAIN

Questions

1 What kind of a person is Percival?

2 Explain how Sir Jasper could be called a 'cruel monster'.

3 What evidence can you find to show that Fanny loves Percival?

4 Why does Sir Jasper offer to take Fanny to The Hall with him?

5 What is Ma Adams's reaction to Sir Jasper's offer?

6 Describe how Sir Jasper is 'foiled'.

7 In what ways is Percival's wife different from Fanny?

8 What are some of the happenings that are not believable?

9 Why does Fanny decide to accept Sir Jasper in marriage?

10 How would you play the part of **(a)** Sir Jasper? **(b)** Fanny? **(c)** Fanny's grandmother?

MY FAIR MACBETH

Larry Pigram

Introduction

Shakespeare's Macbeth, despite his failings and his ultimate tragedy, was a Scottish monarch. Our Macbeth is a lowly figure. He is a mere 'garbo' struggling to win the hand of the fair Morphelia. His social status is his problem, and like Shakespeare's Macbeth, with the aid of the three witches, he improves his position in his environment. He rises to the exalted position of a plumber.

This revue sketch, like most revue sketches, is pliable and additions and cuts may be made to suit the particular class and situation. There are three sections which can be adapted to music if the need or desire arises. In the classroom situation, these sections should be read as part of the play.

Cast

Macbeth
Banquo
Morphelia
Macduffer
Witch I
Witch II
Witch III

SCENE I

*(A garbage dump. **Macbeth** is unloading rubbish. He wears Shakespearian dress except for navy singlet and cap. Enter **Banquo** dressed in the same manner. Both speak with heavy Aussie accents.)*

Banquo   Hail Macbeth, greetings and salutations!
    (aside) That is, I'm sure you'll be knowing,
    Nothing but Shakespeare talk for 'How ya going?'

Macbeth   Ah, Banquo, I fear I must say
    That this has been a pig of a day.

Banquo   Pray tell, Macca, answer this question.
    Is the reason racing, cops or indigestion?

Macbeth   Neither, Banquo. I have been bitten by the love-bug.

Banquo   How can this be, Macbeth? I feel you hurt my pride.
    I'm sure the garbo truck's been sprayed with insecticide.

Macbeth   'Tis not that sort of bug, dear Banquo. I want to wed the
    sweet Morphelia.

Banquo   Ah, yes, Morphelia.
A bad choice, Macbeth!
(aside) She's been wed before and as I betook it,
Though she can dish it out, she sure can't cook it.

Macbeth   Banquo, dost thou not like her?

Banquo   Oh, methinks she doth grow on you.
(aside) Like a wart!

Macbeth   But I fear our love will be but a farce,
For she will not marry below her class.
My hopes for marriage could not be number
'Cause she's the daughter of the local plumber.

Banquo   *(aside)* Yes, his love has suffered a mortal blow,
For no plumber's daughter would marry a garbo!

Macbeth   But I have a plan to overcome this hitch,
I have invented something to make me rich.

Banquo   Pray tell, Macca, what it is?

Macbeth   It's a super duper psychedelic trash and garbage crusher!

(This could be sung to the tune of 'Supercalifragilisticexpialidocious' from Mary Poppins.)

Super duper psychedelic trash and garbage crusher.
Even though the noise it makes is something sure to hush ya,
If you fill it full enough, you're sure to get a gusher.
Super duper psychedelic trash and garbage crusher.

'Cause I always shirk my work and money never had,
Morphelia gave my face a slap and told me I'm a cad.
But then one day I made a thing to save my aching face
The biggest bin you've ever seen to put her in her place.

CHORUS

I'll labour through the day and night and save every cent
And fill my bin until they say I am a worthy gent.
When toffs and proper ladies come and seek my company,
I'll tell my Morphelia and she's sure to marry me.

CHORUS *(with gusto)*

SCENE II

*(**Morphelia** and her dad, **Macduffer**, sitting together. **Macduffer** is studying a racing form while **Morphelia** plays a lute.)*

Morphelia Pray, father, what are you doing?

Macduffer That which doth make every Aussie heart warm,
Picking winners from a racing form.
But now I am full of windy belches,
Pray go make a few Alka-Seltzers.

Morphelia Just a mo' father. How goes the horses?

Macduffer I know something that my heart it touches,
For I could beat them all on crutches.

(Puts head in his hands.)

A horse! A horse! My kingdom for a horse.

Morphelia *(aside)* You see losing at the races doth get my father
where it hurteth most — in the wallet!
But come father take my lute and tune her,
While I go and pour you a schooner.

Macduffer Ah, you are so understanding, my daughter dear
To keep at home a fridge full of beer.

Morphelia Hark! What noise is that?

(Rattle offstage.)

Tins that rattle and flies that hum
Means but one thing — Macbeth doth come.

*(Enter **Macbeth** carrying a garbage bin on one shoulder.)*

Macbeth *(rushing to **Morphelia**)* Ah, Morphelia my sweet sheilah!

Morphelia *(backing away)* Oh, Macbeth, pray leave this hearth
At least until thou hath a bath.

Macbeth *(hurt)* Morphelia!

Morphelia Macbeth thou never my heart will win
Whilst thou causest my head to spin.

And while with garbage your truck you load her,
You'll never get rid of that terrible odour.

Macbeth   But pray, Morphelia, what is the matter with my job?

Morphelia   Macbeth, I know a garbo's lot is not a happy one
But the smell of your truck doth really stun.
In truth, I say, I tell you no wrong
Just listen a while to this little song.

(This next section could be sung to the tune of 'Oh What A Beautiful Morning' from Oklahoma!*)*

There's a real dirty haze round a garbo.
There's a real dirty haze round a garbo.
The truck's piled as high as an Aussie meat pie,
And it looks like it's reaching clear up to the sky.

Oh what a terrible odour. Oh what a terrible trade.
I've got a terrible feeling th'whole lot's coming my way.

Oh the noise of the truck is so deaf'ning.
Oh the noise of the truck is so deaf'ning.
It makes me so dizzy, I must make a plea.
And my poor little daddy don't know what it be.

Oh what a terrible odour. Oh what a terrible trade.
I've got a terrible feeling th'whole lot's coming my way.
Oh what a terrible trade.

SCENE III

(Garbage dump. Three witches are sitting round cauldron throwing trash into it.)

Witch I   Round about the cauldron go,
In the empty beer cans throw.
Fish that in the 'Telegraph'
Hath days and nights twelve and a half.
Uncleaned carcass of rabbit shot
Boil thou first in the charmed pot.

Witch II   Double, double toil and trouble;
Fire, burn; and, chewing-gum, bubble.

Witch III   Dry remains of some old cake
In the cauldron boil and bake.
Head of fish and legs of frogs
Cricket bat and someone's togs.
Bended fork and yo-yo string
And some records crooned by Bing.

Witch II   Double, double toil and trouble;
Fire, burn; and, chewing-gum, bubble.

*(Enter **Macbeth**.)*

Macbeth   What strange creatures meet I here
Perhaps visions from too much beer?
No! No! My mind's not giddy
For all I had was but a middy.

Witches   All hail Macbeth!

Macbeth   How can it be, this strange greeting?
'Tis not what I'm used to at first meeting.

Witch I   Perhaps you are wary of our chatter?
But proper let me greet you — how ya goin', Macca?

Macbeth   And now a proper greeting let me deal ya's;
An old Aussie welcome — how ya goin', sheilahs?
But pray, what is the purpose of your visit?

Witch II   We tell a secret that will surely numb ya.
For you're the long-lost son of a Scottish plumber.

Macbeth   But what dost this mean?

Witch III   A good hand it seems the fates did deal ya,
For now you can marry your Morphelia.

Macbeth   But I still can marry her?

Witch I   But pray, why not you rotten dingo?
You look as if you'd lost at Bingo.

Macbeth   I fear though a plumber may be my status,
My accent's as Aussie as baked potatoes.

Witch II   But I can fix that quite readily
All you do is repeat after me.

(This could be sung to the tune of 'The Rain in Spain Stays Mainly in the Plain' from My Fair Lady.)

The rain, it's plain, goes mainly down the drain.

Macbeth   The rain, it's plain, goes mainly down the drain.

Witch III   Again!

Macbeth   The rain, it's plain, goes mainly down the drain.

Witch I   I think he's got it! I think he's got it!

Macbeth   The rain, it's plain, goes mainly down the drain.

Witch II   By Hecate, he's got it! By Hecate, he's got it!

(Repeat main line three times with gusto.)

Witch III   And where does it rain?

Macbeth   Down the drain! Down the drain!

Witch I   And where's that blasted drain?

Macbeth   *(pointing to spot on ground)* It's plain! It's plain!

All   Oh the rain, it's plain, goes mainly down the drain.

(Big finish.)

All   Yes, the rain, it's plain, goes mainly down the drain.

SCENE IV

*(**Morphelia** playing her lute. Enter **Macbeth**, dressed rather elegantly.)*

Macbeth   *(in very cultured accent)* Ah, my sweet Morphelia.

Morphelia   Macbeth? It is you, my gosh.
How is it you sound so very posh?

Macbeth   'Tis in keeping with my new job, Morphelia.

(Opens bag.)

Canst thou see by this monkey wrench
That my job will no longer cause a stench?
For a garbo no longer will I be,
But a plumber now for all to see.

Morphelia   One moment, wait Macbeth, my dear,
While I call my father from his beer.

Macduffer   *(enters)* I heard it all sweet Morphelia.

Macbeth   How say you Macduffer?

*(Takes **Morphelia's** hand.)*

Macduffer It looks as though you've won this little number.
(*aside*) I'm not losing a daughter, but gaining a plumber.

(*Enter* **Banquo** *and the* **Witches**.)

Morphelia Now that everyone's here, I have a confession, Macca.

Macbeth Pray tell, my sweet passion-flower.

Morphelia I discovered only lately, my dear Macca,
That my beloved's profession does not matter.
Thus if thou wouldst still have me,
As a garbo I will wed thee.

Macbeth Ah, Morphelia thou saddens me.

Morphelia Why dear soul?

Macbeth By your confession so heart-rending
Thou hast wrecked up our planned ending.
But since thou lovest me with such force
We'll let the play run its course.

Macduffer, **Banquo**, **Witches** (*all together*)
Thus like all good plays, ours ended happily
In the tradition of Snow White, and Lady Chatterley.
The principals wed, the cast well fed,
All villainy dead, and soon children to be bred.
But all critics would declare our play to pong,
If we didn't include another song.
So settle back and take a breath
And listen to Morphelia and Macbeth.

Macbeth and **Morphelia** 'Garbo Callin'.

(*This could be sung to the tune of 'Oklahoma!'. With great gusto.*)

Gaaaarrr-bo callin' and the truck comes roaring down the street,
And the week-old meat will sure smell sweet
When the truck's piled high with Aussie trash.
Gaaaaarrr-bo callin', every day my sugar-plum and I,
Drive along the road, and watch the load
Building castles right up to the sky.

We know we belong to the trade,
And the trade we belong to's not staid;
And when we say hip, oh hip! Oh hip hooray;
Oh hip, oh hip! — we're only thinking:
You're going fine garbage dealer,
Garbage dealer, garbo!

(Repeat with gusto, at the end adding:)

G—A—R—B—O—B—O, garbage dealer —
Yo!!

CURTAIN

Questions

1   The title 'My Fair Macbeth' suggests some kind of comparison with the musical *My Fair Lady*. See what similarities you can find in your reading of the play.

2   Macbeth wishes to marry the sweet Morphelia. What obstacle stands in his way?

3   How does he propose to overcome it?

4   What objections does Banquo have to Morphelia?

5   The rhyming couplet (a pair of successive lines which rhyme with each other) such as:

'Ah, Banquo, I fear I must say
That this has been a pig of a day.'

is used with great effect in the play. Quote three that really make you laugh.

6   Give an example of a humorous misunderstanding between Macbeth and Banquo from Scene I.

7   According to Morphelia, what two things always herald the approach of Macbeth?

8   The original witches' chant from Shakespeare's *Macbeth* goes:

'Double, double toil and trouble;
Fire, burn; and, cauldron, bubble.'

What change has Larry Pigram made to this?

9 Can you say why this change adds humour?

10 In your opinion, what is the most hilarious object tossed into the cauldron by the witches?

11 'The rain in Spain stays mainly in the plain' is the original line from George Bernard Shaw's *Pygmalion* (the play on which *My Fair Lady* was based). What change has Larry Pigram made?

12 Why does this change add humour?

13 Complete the comparisons:
(a) Morphelia grows on you like . . .
(b) The truck's piled as high as . . .
(c) My accent's as Aussie as . . .

14 According to the cast, all good plays have four ingredients for a happy ending. What are they?

15 'But all critics would declare our play to pong', we are told. Explain the double meaning involved here.

16 How is the humour created in *My Fair Macbeth*? (Think about slang, dignity, contrast, mental pictures called up.)

MEN OF MAGNET

Larry Pigram

Introduction

Men of Magnet is a send-up of the television series, *Dragnet*. In *Dragnet* the two policemen were always tough and rugged and by clever analysis and their own intuition never failed to get their man. The situation was tense, serious and full of suspense. On the other hand, our two heroes of *Men of Magnet* are quite the reverse. They try to be tough and heroic, but are made to appear foolish by their own remarks and the situations in which they find themselves.

Cast

Narrator
Sam Sunday..................A detective
Kelly.............................Another detective
Bank Manager
Girl...............................An accountant in a bank
Suspect
Policeman

SCENE

Police headquarters. **Sam Sunday** *and his associate* **Kelly** *are on stage. However, before the curtain opens, the* **Narrator** *comes out in front of the curtain. The theme from* Dragnet *is heard in the background.*

Narrator The people you are about to see are true. Only the story has been changed to protect the innocent.

(The curtain opens to reveal **Sam** *and* **Kelly** *sitting at a table with a phone next to them.)*

Sam This is the city. There are two million people in the city. It's a big city. When any of these two million people step out of line, they call me. My name is Sunday. Sam Sunday. I'm a cop. The time is 8.59 and 59 seconds and I'm expecting a call at any moment now. *(The phone rings.)* At 9.00 the phone rang. At 9.00.01 I picked up the phone. *(He picks up the phone.)* At 9.00.02 I said, 'Hullo'. *(He says 'Hullo'.)* Yes, madam. Just give me the facts, madam. Just give me the facts, madam. Right, thank you, madam.

Kelly   *(He picks up his hat.)* What is it, Sam? Another case for the 'Men of Magnet'? Right?

Sam   Wrong! It was my mother. It's raining and she wants to know if I remembered to shut the back door. *(The* Dragnet *music breaks in.)* At 9.04 Mother called to say that she had dropped three stitches on the sweater she was knitting me. At 9.06 we received a report of a bank robbery. At 9.08 the bank manager was brought in for questioning. *(A **policeman** brings in the **bank manager**.)* Sir, would you tell us the amount taken?

Manager   Just a moment. I have a list. *(He takes out a list.)* Ah, yes. He took 100 000 dollars, a female accountant and two boxes of Smarties.

Kelly   Could you describe the girl for me?

Manager   Not really. All I can say is that she was very efficient in her work.

Sam   Could you describe the robber?

Manager   Yes. I got a good look at him. He was heavy-set with a slight build. Short, but looked taller than he really was. Good teeth but badly decayed and prominent features with a flat face.

Sam   That's a pretty accurate description. Have a scar?

Manager   No thanks, I don't smoke.

Sam   Did he have a moustache?

Manager   I'm not sure. But if he has one he sure keeps it shaved off. (Dragnet *music*.)

Sam   9.30. Mother called to tell me she had picked up the stitches on my sweater.
9.35. Made hurried visit to cafeteria.
11.35. Arrived back from cafeteria.
11.40. The phone rang.

Kelly   Hullo . . . yes . . . yes. (*Aside*.) Sam, the boys have just brought in a woman who was found wandering around French's Forest. They want to know what to do with her.

Sam   Hold her for questioning. (Dragnet *music*.) Have just received a report of a female accountant wandering through French's Forest. Ordered her brought in for questioning. (*A **girl** is brought in*.) Sit down, my dear. It must have been quite an ordeal for you.

Girl   Oh, yes, it was horrible.

Sam   You poor girl. What happened?

Girl   Well, we were driving along the Pacific Highway when the car suddenly stopped.

Sam   You clonked the cowardly cad with a crowbar?

Girl   Nope!

Sam   You banged the baseless bounder in the belly?

Girl   Nope!

Sam   You mashed the mooching milksop with a meatball?

Girl   Wrong again. We ran out of petrol?

Sam   Ah! Then, you escaped?

Girl   Right, at last.

Sam   How do I know you are telling the truth?

Girl   No, that's true.

Kelly   *(aside)* I'll test her, Sam. *(To the* **girl***.)* What would you do if you found 100 000 dollars lying in the street?

Girl   If it belonged to a poor family, I'd give it back. *(Dragnet music. The* **girl** *is taken outside.)*

Sam   11.50. Made hurried exit to have lunch.
3.50. Returned from lunch.
4.00. Suspect brought in for questioning. *(**Suspect** is brought in struggling.)* Your full name, please.

Suspect   Peter Rabbit the Third.

Sam   Come off it. You can't play games with me.

Suspect   What do you mean?

Sam   Do you expect me to believe your name is Peter Rabbit the Third?

Suspect   Why not?

Sam   I happen to know Peter Rabbit the Third.

Suspect OK. I admit it. He's my father. I'm Peter Rabbit the Fourth.

Sam That's better. Now what do you say to the charges laid against you?

Suspect If I confess, will you make sure that I'm treated fairly?

Sam Certainly. You'll have all the advantages of the jury system. You'll get a fair and merciful trial. But before you do I'd like to ask you one question.

Suspect Yes, sir?

Sam What voltage do you prefer, AC or DC?

Suspect I deny everything!

Sam Oh, come now. You have a record as long as your arm. *(He takes out paper.)* It says here that you stole 200 000 dollars when you were nineteen? Why did you do it?

Suspect   My father was out of work.

Kelly   Listen to me, you. Sam may talk like a fool, act like a fool and look like a fool. But don't be deceived. He really is a fool.

Sam   Thank you, Kelly.

Kelly   That's all right, sir.

Sam   Frisk him, Kelly.

Kelly   *(He frisks the **suspect** and reaches into his inside pocket.)* Aha!

Sam   What did you find?

Kelly   Three Smarties. *(He hands them to **Sam**.)*

Sam   We have you now. I charge you with grand larceny and kidnapping.

Suspect   You can't pin that on me. I won't take no rap for no-one. It's a frame-up, you dirty rotten cop.

Sam   Well, if that charge fails, we've got you on a '973'.

Suspect   A '973'? What's a '973'?

Sam   Overacting!

CURTAIN

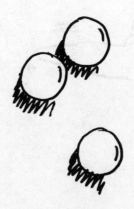

Questions

1   What comment would you make on the unusual title?

2   What true-to-life touch does the constant reporting of the time add to the play?

3   The phone calls received by Sam add to the play's humour. Why?

4   The tough, shrewd, intelligent detective image becomes somewhat tarnished in Sam's case. How?

5   'That's a pretty accurate description', says Sam in response to information given by the bank manager. Say why you would find it hard to agree.

6   'Sling me a salami sandwich, Sam' is an example of alliteration — the repetition of initial consonants in a 'run' of words. You must admit it has some interesting sound-effects. Find three examples of alliteration in the play.

7   Explain how the girl 'shows up' both the detectives.

8   What does Sam mean by, 'What voltage do you prefer, AC or DC?'?

9   How does this fit in with what Sam has just told the suspect?

10   Kelly makes an outstandingly honest statement. Find it.

11   Would this be an easy or a hard play to produce? Give reasons for your answer.

12   Briefly explain why you feel that the dramatist was successful or unsuccessful.

Larry Pigram

Cast
Announcer
Tarzan
Jane
Marriage Counsellor

SCENE I

Tarzan and *Jane* at home.

Announcer   In the movies and on television Tarzan, with great courage and resourcefulness, has been righting all kinds of injustices — stopping slave traders, preventing the wholesale slaughter of the jungle animals, fighting with crocodiles, rescuing helpless white men or white women from the clutches of hostile natives, etc. His marriage with Jane has been seen as an example of marital bliss. However, now we are to be given new insights into Tarzan's domestic affairs.

Our first scene shows Tarzan and Jane spending a night at home together in their tree house.

(Tarzan and Jane are seated on the lounge. Tarzan reads paper, while Jane knits.)

Tarzan   Watcha wanna do tonight, Jane?

Jane   I dunno, Tarzan, what do you wanna do?

Tarzan   Nothin' much . . . whatever you wanna do.

Jane   I don't wanna do nothin' . . . whatta you wanna do?

Tarzan   Nothin'.

Jane   Oh. *(Few seconds silence.)*

Tarzan   Watcha say we amble down to the campfire and see who's cookin'?

Jane   Nah! *(Few seconds silence.)*

Tarzan   Anything exciting happen today?

Jane   *(still knitting)* Mrs Sambo's son got expelled from cannibal school today.

Tarzan   *(not really interested)* What for?

Jane   Buttering up too many teachers.

Tarzan   Yeh?

Jane   Yeh.

Tarzan   Oh.

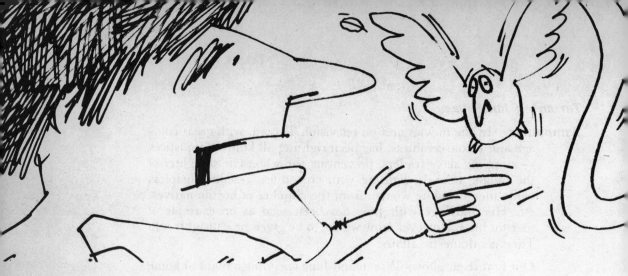

Jane   Anything exciting happen at the soccer?

Tarzan   Yeh.

Jane   What?

Tarzan   The Watsui Wanderers beat the Zulu Hotspurs 107 to 0.

Jane   What happened to the Hotspurs?

Tarzan   Crocodile took their goalie.

Jane   Yeh?

Tarzan   Yeh.

Jane   Anything else happen?

Tarzan   Yeh. Old chief Zum Zum told me a joke.

Jane   Yeh?

Tarzan   Yeh.

Jane   What is it?

Tarzan   What's green on the inside, white on the outside and hops?

Jane   I dunno. What is green on the inside, white on the outside and hops?

Tarzan   A frog sandwich!

Jane   *(not amused)* Yeh?

Tarzan   Yeh. *(Few seconds silence.)*

Jane   Mrs Hoho has gone on a diet.

Tarzan   Yeh?

Jane   Eats nothing but coconuts.

Tarzan   Lose any weight?

Jane   Not a pound . . . but you should see her climb a tree. *(Silence.)*

Tarzan   I had to shoot Rover this morning.

Jane   That's too bad . . . Was he mad?

Tarzan   Well, he wasn't exactly pleased.

Jane   *(changing the subject)* Tarzan, why don't you pull your stomach in?

Tarzan   *(hurt)* I have.

Jane   Getting a bit of a paunch, aren't you?

Tarzan   *(angry)* You look a million.

Jane   Thank you.

Tarzan   And I mean every year of it.

Jane   Oh, yeh?

Tarzan   Anyway, it's your cooking that does it.

Jane   What's up with my cooking?

Tarzan   You're the only woman who rinses ice cubes in hot water and then goes crook because she can't find them.

Jane   Look. Why don't you tell me what I said that has made you so annoyed . . . It might come in handy again some time.

Tarzan   I'm sorry Jane.

Jane   Really?

Tarzan   Yeh.

Jane   Then, I'm sorry too.

Tarzan   Thanks. *(Few seconds silence.)*

Jane   Tarzan, do you realize it's my birthday today?

Tarzan   Yeh?

Jane   Yeh.

Tarzan   Whatta you wanna do to celebrate?

Jane   I dunno . . . whatta you wanna do?

(Curtains start slowly to close.)

Tarzan   Whatever you wanna do.

Jane   I don't wanna do nothing . . . what ever you wanna do.

(Both keep going until the curtain closes.)

SCENE II

Tarzan and *Jane* visit the **Marriage Counsellor**.

Announcer   Tarzan and Jane, because of their matrimonial problems, decide to visit the marriage counsellor.

Marriage Counsellor   Have you any complaints to make, Tarzan?

Tarzan   Well, I don't like the way Jane wakes me up in the morning. She throws the cat at me.

Marriage Counsellor   What's wrong with that?

Tarzan   I sleep with the dog.

Marriage Counsellor   I see . . . any other complaints?

Tarzan   Well, I don't like her cooking.

Jane   Look, I don't understand you. I give you papaws on Monday night and you like 'em. Papaws on Wednesday night and you like 'em. Papaws on Thursday night and you like 'em. Then for some reason on Friday night, you don't like papaws.

Marriage Counsellor   Jane, I understand that you have decided to file a divorce order. Why?

Jane   Well, I was quite ill a while back and the doctor said I needed some sea air and do you know what my stingy husband did?

Marriage Counsellor   No.

Jane   For two weeks he fanned me with a dead herring.

CURTAIN

Questions

1 What is humorous about the setting of this play?

2 A pun is a play on words, usually involving double meaning. Give several examples of punning by **(a)** Jane, **(b)** Tarzan.

3 Another form of humour in the play is based on the unexpected ending:

> '*Tarzan*   You look a million.
> *Jane*   Thank you.
> *Tarzan*   And I mean every year of it.'

Give several more examples of this kind of humour.

4 What criticism does Jane make of Tarzan's physique?

5 How does Tarzan twist the blame onto Jane?

6 In what humorous way does Tarzan show that Jane lacks common sense?

7 Find an example of Jane's lack of understanding of Tarzan's daily needs.

8 Why does Jane call her husband 'stingy'?

9 What is left in the play of the old Tarzan and Jane of movie fame?

a villa on venus.

Kenneth Lillington

Cast

Sham Gimble	} .... Citizens of the Planet Venus
Frank Fearless Bill Bold Dick Dreadnought	} .. Visitors from the Planet Earth
Spiv	A salesman from the Planet Mercury
First B.E.M. Second B.E.M. Third B.E.M. Fourth B.E.M. Fifth B.E.M. Sixth B.E.M.	} .... Bug-Eyed Monsters

SCENE

The curtain rises on a landscape in northern Venus which, though distinctly unworldly, is not unfamiliar to us, for we have seen similar scenes often enough on the covers of science-fiction magazines. The background is a conglomeration of futuristic machinery and exotic vegetation. Down left is an equally futuristic seat, and up right, a Reflector, which resembles a large shaving-mirror mounted on a revolving stand. Into this **Sham** *is gazing intently.*

Sham   Gimble!

Gimble   *(off-stage, left)* Yes, guv?

Sham   Come here a minute, will you?

Gimble   *(off-stage)* All right, I'm coming.

> *(Enter* **Gimble***. He and* **Sham***, whose flesh is a bright golden colour, are both dressed in simple Grecian tunics.* **Sham***, much the older of the two, is a genial little creature, cultured in voice, kindly and worldly-wise in manner.* **Gimble** *is young, brisk, efficient; and he speaks, curiously enough, in a strong cockney accent.)*

Gimble   What is it? Someone landing?

Sham   Yes, and I don't like the look of it. Take a look in the reflector, Gimble, will you? Your eyes are better than mine.

> *(He crosses to the seat, left.)*

Gimble   *(manipulating the reflector)* Can't see a thing . . . Ah, wait a bit, though. Yes, I can.

Sham   Where are they from, that's the point?

Gimble   Hard to say. Not Jupiter.

Sham   No.

Gimble   Not Mars, either.

Sham   No.

Gimble Well, really, I've never seen a crate like this before. Looks as if it's come out of the Ark. In fact, I'm not sure it *isn't* the Ark . . . Do you know, it may sound crazy, but —

Sham Well?

Gimble I think they're from the Earth!

Sham *(grimly)* Exactly! The Red Planet.

Gimble Oh, but they couldn't be. They're living in the Dark Ages down there!

Sham That's no argument. It'd be just like them to invent some fantastic craft centuries after all the other planets have done it, and then think themselves lords of the Universe. What do you bet me they start offering us coloured beads when they get here?

Gimble They might not get here! You should see this thing rocking about!

Sham   Well, I wish them no harm, but I don't like this. I've watched the Earth through the instrument for years, and I wouldn't exactly call the natives friendly.

Gimble   Act rather queer, don't they?

Sham   They're raving mad, my son. They keep blowing one another to bits.

Gimble   Oh, well, that's all right, then. They'll blow one another to bits, and we'll go on living our dignified lives.

Sham   No, you don't quite understand. What I mean is —

Gimble   *(with a shout)* They're through! They're going to land! . . . Easy, now, Earthmen. Gently does it . . . Nose her down . . . Steady, steady . . . Blimey! They're going to crash!

(He dives off, left, in alarm, with **Sham** *after him. From off-stage right there is an ear-splitting crash, several rolling echoes, and a series of flashes. The faces of* **Sham** *and* **Gimble** *appear cautiously from the wings.)*

Gimble   What a rotten landing!

Sham   Sh! Here they come.

(They withdraw their heads. Enter **Frank Fearless**, **Dick Dreadnought**, *and* **Bill Bold**, *tugging off their space-helmets. Their dress is as familiar as the scenery: for they are wearing the space-suits we have seen so often in magazines and on the screen. They place their helmets on the ground, well to the rear, stretch, and inhale deeply.)*

Frank   Thank goodness to get that thing off! Some fool cleaned the inside with paraffin!

Dick   Awfully hot, isn't it?

Bill   *(waving an arm at the scenery)* We're in the South, I imagine.

Sham   *(off-stage)* Lucky for you you're not!

Frank   Strange! I thought I heard a voice!

Dick   So did I.

Bill   An echo, no doubt.

Dick   Now that's just silly. You said, 'We're in the South, I imagine.' How could that echo back as 'Lucky for you you're not'?

Gimble   *(off-stage)* Shows he's thinking, anyway.

Frank   *(casting an eye over the immensely complicated machinery in the background)* It's possible, I suppose, that there may be *life* here, in a primitive form.

Sham   *(off-stage)* Thank you, sir.

Dick   There it is again — that sound!

Bill   *(resolutely)* I'm going to investigate this!

Sham   *(emerging, followed by **Gimble**)* Don't bother. Good evening, gentlemen.

Frank   Good Lord! Things from Another World!

Gimble   *(irritated)* Cheek! Who got here first?

Dick   It speaks English!

Bill   *(roaring with laughter)* Ha, ha, ha! Look at its face!

Frank   Steady, fellows. I shall try to speak to it. Er — greetings, creatures.

Sham   Greetings to you. Have a toffee.

Dick   Steady, Frank. May be poisoned.

Frank   No, no. We must humour them. Er — how does one eat this sort of thing?

Gimble   Well, one puts it in one's mouth, one moves one's jaws about, and finally one swallows.

Frank   *(with dignity)* I see. And now — how is it that you are speaking English?

Sham   *(to **Gimble**, with a gesture of resignation)* Oh, it's like talking to a savage! *(to **Frank**)* Well, you see, the air here is charged with rays which turn our thoughts into a common language. To you, I may seem to be speaking English — to me, you seem to be speaking *my* language.

Frank   Ah, I see. We have something of the sort on the Earth.

Dick   It's called United Nations.

Sham   If it isn't a personal question, why have you come to Venus?

Frank   Ah, Venus has always lured Man.

Dick   We are here in the name of Progress.

Sham   Oh. We're here in the name of *(introducing **Gimble**)* Gimble, and *(bowing)* Sham. *(He points to the ray-guns which the **Earthmen** are holding.)* And what are those?

Bill   *(flourishing gun)* These are ray-guns. They can blow an elephant to bits at a distance of two miles.

Gimble   And you've got those in the name of Progress, too, I suppose?

Frank   Yes, of course. The natives must be shown who is their master. But don't worry — you seem friendly little beings. We shan't shoot you.

Gimble   That's very kind of you.

Frank   We are driven by an insatiable craving for Progress. All our race have this urge. We are the first Men on Venus, but soon, others will come, spurred by our example —

Sham   How delightful!

Frank   They will overrun the Solar System. They will embrace the great nebulae. They will take the sun.

Gimble   Well, be careful where you take it, mate. It's useful.

Dick   *(eagerly)* Frank's right. Before long, every housewife on the Earth will own a villa on Venus.

Gimble   And what about us?

Bill   Ah, to you will fall the honour of being Man's first interplanetary assistants.

Sham   Well, well, well . . . Anyway, it's a good job you didn't land in the South.

Dick   So you said before. Why?

Sham   The B.E.Ms live in the South.

Frank   B.E.Ms?

Gimble   The B.E.Ms — the Bug-Eyed Monsters.

Frank   Come, come! Bug-Eyed Monsters exist only in the cheapest fiction.

Sham   I'm afraid life's rather like the cheapest fiction, my boy.

Bill   But what are they like — the B.E.Ms?

Gimble   Cor — like nothing on Earth.

Sham   But don't worry. They never come here.

Dick   Now that's a pity. These creatures must be most interesting phenomena. We might have got some pictures of them.

Gimble   *(furiously)* Look, mate; the B.E.Ms are not going to pose for you while you tell 'em to watch the birdy! They're really nasty, those things are, and we don't want 'em here, see?

Frank   Well, they don't come here anyway, according to you.

Gimble   You never know. *They* might want to take pictures of *you*.

Sham Come, this is getting us nowhere. I think that before you gentlemen make any more — er — progress, you'd better have some supper.

Gimble It won't be poison. We don't eat poison.

Sham Come, Gimble. Sit down, gentlemen. We'll call you when supper's ready.

(*Exit* **Sham** *and* **Gimble**. *The* **Earthmen** *sit on the seat, left.*)

Frank Quaint little creatures, aren't they? Almost human.

Dick Very simple-minded, though.

Bill Oh, rather. What stuff about Bug-Eyed Monsters!

(*Enter, left, a* **Bug-Eyed Monster**. *It wears a long green cloak, black tights, and a green hood, from which stares a green and demoniac face. Grinning wickedly, it lurks behind the* **Earthmen**, *listening as they chat.*)

Dick Pure children's-comic stuff!

Frank Oh, I entirely agree. I for one don't believe in the B.E.Ms for a moment.

(*The* **B.E.M.** *moves silently to centre, and beckons. Enter five more* **B.E.Ms**, *exactly like the first, from right. They form a line, centre to right. The* **First B.E.M.** *stands downstage, a little apart from the others.*)

Dick I intend to write an article about the childish beliefs of the beings on Venus.

Bill I wonder if this supper's ready? I expect — (*in consternation*) Hey! Look, chaps — look!

(*The* **Earthmen** *spring to their feet, see the* **B.E.Ms** *and back away apprehensively.*)

First B.E.M. Greetings, Earthmen!

Frank (*gulping*) Er-yes, of course. Greetings.

First B.E.M.   We observed your arrival, and hurried here to greet you.

Dick   V-very good of you.

First B.E.M.   Good? Please don't use that unpleasant language here. We despise goodness.

Bill   But what do you want to do?

B.E.Ms   *(exultantly)* WE WORK FOR THE DESTRUCTION OF MANKIND.

Second B.E.M.   *(stepping forward)* Yes. For many years we have had visitors to Venus from other planets — Mercury, Mars, Jupiter, Saturn. But they have all been creatures of peace, and have used their science to keep us away. Always have we turned our longing eyes on your planet, for you and we — ah! we can work together so beautifully for the death of man!

B.E.Ms   *(joyfully)* DEATH! THE DEATH OF MAN!

Third B.E.M.   *(stepping forward)* For your planet, the red planet, Earth, is the planet of Murder and Death.

B.E.Ms   MURDER AND DEATH!

Fourth B.E.M.   *(stepping forward)* Join us, Earthmen, in our great plan to destroy Mankind!

Fifth B.E.M.   *(stepping forward)* Help us to launch the avalanche of our rage!

Sixth B.E.M.   *(stepping foward)* Haste with us to the Day of Doom!

B.E.Ms   DOOM!

*(But the **Earthmen** are extremely indignant.)*

Frank   Now look here, you rotten blighters — you've got us all wrong!

Bill   We wouldn't dream of joining your disgusting plot.

Dick   You can jolly well put your hands up, and don't try any tricks, because these guns can blow an elephant to bits at two miles!

First B.E.M.   Ha ha! *(To the others.) Hypnotize* these men!

(*The **B.E.Ms** swing their arms rhythmically, crooning as they do so — Whoo . . . Whoo . . . Bonk! — and at the 'bonk' the **Earthmen** are struck rigid.*)

First B.E.M.   Excellent! Now, in their trance, they will tell us all the secrets of their life on Earth! Right, men — On to Doom!

B.E.Ms   ON TO DOOM!

(*They file out, leaving the **Earthmen** still transfixed. The last **B.E.M.** puts his head round the curtain.*)

B.E.M.   Er — follow us, please.

(*Arms outstretched like sleepwalkers, the **Earthmen** follow. Re-enter **Sham** and **Gimble**, who carries a tray with three covered dishes on it.*)

Sham   Well, here you are, gents . . . Well! where have they gone to?

Gimble   Gone exploring, maybe. *(He sets down the tray.)*

Sham   After all our trouble, too. What bad manners.

Gimble *(sniffing the air)* Just a minute. Can you smell something?

Sham *(sniffing)* Yes, now that you mention it.

Gimble Rather like sulphur, isn't it?

Sham Yes, it is rather —

> *(They stare at each other, suddenly.)*

Sham and **Gimble** *(together)* Sulphur!

Sham *(greatly alarmed)* The B.E.Ms have got them!

Gimble Talk about birds of a feather!

Sham *(sitting down)* I suppose we ought to rescue them.

Gimble *(joining him on the seat)* Yes . . . We'll start tomorrow, shall we?

Sham Hallo! *(pointing into wings, right)* There's someone coming.

Gimble Why, it's that salesman fellow from Mercury. It's old Spiv. Hi-ya, Spiv!

> *(Enter **Spiv**. He is dressed like **Sham** and **Gimble**, and resembles them, but that he looks old and very weary. He lugs an enormous suitcase.)*

Sham *(going forward to shake his hand)* Hallo, Spiv! I haven't seen you for ages!

Gimble *(with sympathy)* You look a bit done up, cocker. Come and sit down and rest your feet.

> *(**Spiv** sinks down, planting the suitcase at his feet.)*

Spiv That's the way I feel. *(without hope)* You don't want to buy a death-ray, do you?

Sham No, thank you.

Spiv It'll wipe out a whole city.

Sham Well, when I want to wipe out a whole city, I'll remember you.

Spiv *(dejectedly)* They all talk like that nowadays.

Gimble Business is bad, is it mate?

Spiv Terrible. I go up and down the Solar System, calling on all the planets until I'm worn out, but no one wants to buy weapons any more. Peace and concord — nothing but peace and concord wherever I go. It's awful.

Gimble Not very nice, though, is it, selling things that kill people?

Spiv What can I do? It's my bread and butter. I suppose I could get another job, but that's not easy at my time of life.

Sham You might sell to the B.E.Ms.

Spiv *(shocked)* Oh, no, no. I've got some conscience left.

Sham Well — who don't you try the Earth?

Spiv *(considering)* The planet Earth? ... No, not worth bothering about. They're too backward. *(He rises wearily.)* The fact is, I'm finished. *(He picks up his case and walks to centre.)* They just don't want machines of death any more. Books of poetry now — they sell like hot cakes.

Sham I do wish I could help you, Spiv.

Spiv I know you would if you could, old chap.

Gimble Perhaps a lovely war will break out somewhere. Keep your chin up.

Spiv No such luck. But thanks for listening. So long, fellows.

Sham and **Gimble** *(together)* So long, Spiv.

    *(Exit **Spiv**.)*

Gimble Poor old Spiv, selling weapons in a peaceful Universe!

Sham *(gazing after him)* Yes, it's a shame ... What! Some more visitors? *(suddenly)* Gimble! Watch out! It's the B.E.Ms!

    *(**Sham** and **Gimble** take up a defensive position behind the seat as the **B.E.Ms** troop in.)*

Gimble   Now look here — if you want trouble you'll get it. We don't want you nasty things round here!

Sham   Go away!

First B.E.M.   *(anxiously)* No, listen, Sham —

Sham   Sham? Who do you think you're talking to? Get out!

First B.E.M.   No, please listen.

Sham   Oh, all right. What is it?

First B.E.M.   Please help us to get rid of these *ghastly* Earthmen!

Sham   Why, what's wrong with them?

First B.E.M.   *Wrong* with them? They're *unspeakable*.

Gimble   Then why did you kidnap them?

First B.E.M.   Oh, we were in the wrong, we admit it. But we didn't realize that anything could be so vile.

Sham   I thought that you objects worked for 'the destruction of mankind', or something?

First B.E.M.   Yes, yes, but there's a difference between healthy destruction and the horrors we've been told.

Second B.E.M.   We put them in a trance, and they described their life on the Earth.

Third B.E.M.   Their squalid days!

Fourth B.E.M.   Their piggish nights!

Fifth B.E.M.   Their beastly world of business, and their poisonous ways of pleasure!

Sixth B.E.M.   Their repulsive insurance companies, banks and offices!

Second B.E.M.   Their ratlike houses, hotels and clubs!

Third B.E.M.   Their trains and tubes and buses and bicycles!

Fourth B.E.M. Their prisons and palaces and aerodromes and asylums!

Fifth B.E.M. Their luxury liners!

Sixth B.E.M. Their cafes and cinemas!

Second B.E.M. Their picnics on the beach!

Third B.E.M. Their dances on the lawn!

Fourth B.E.M. Their food, beds, funerals, baths!

Fifth B.E.M. Their men!

Sixth B.E.M. Their women!

B.E.Ms *(together)* THEIR BEASTLY LIVES!

First B.E.M. And after all that, what do you think one of them said? I'll tell you. He said, 'In time, every housewife on the Earth will own a villa on Venus!'

Sham *(calmly)* Well, you've really let yourselves in for it this time, haven't you?

First B.E.M. It'll be just as bad for you.

Sham Oh no, it won't. They'll all want to live in the South, you'll see.

  (*B.E.Ms groan.*)

First B.E.M. *(deeply dejected)* Ah, well, we deserve it, I suppose. All right, men — on to Doom!

B.E.Ms *(croaking dismally)* On to Doom.

  (*They begin to shamble away.*)

Sham Wait! I've changed my mind!

B.E.Ms *(returning jubilantly)* Hooray!

Sham Quiet! Gimble, go after Spiv and bring him back, will you?

Gimble Right, guv. (*Exit **Gimble**.*)

First B.E.M.   You're really going to help us?

Sham   Yes. I never thought I'd have any fellow-feeling for a Bug-Eyed Monster, but circumstances alter cases. I'm going to send the Earthmen right back to the Earth.

First B.E.M.   *(advancing with hand outstretched)* This is wonderful! How can I ever thank —

Sham   *(hastily)* Er — keep your distance, please. I don't want to stink of sulphur for the next week.

First B.E.M.   *(retreating)* Oh. Sorry, I'm sure. No offence.

Sham   How soon can you send the Earthmen back to me?

First B.E.M.   At twice the speed of light.

Sham   That'll do. And now go away.

First B.E.M.   With pleasure. What ho, lads, let's sing as we march, shall we?

*(Exit **B.E.Ms**, gaily singing a marching song.)*

Sham   *(advancing to the footlights, to the audience)* I only hope I'm doing the right thing.

*(Re-enter **Gimble** with **Spiv**.)*

Gimble   Here he is, guv'nor.

Sham   Ah, Spiv! I think I might have some business for you after all.

Spiv   That's really handsome of you, Sham.

Sham   Not at all. Got your samples ready?

Spiv   You bet!

Sham   I think you're just about to make your fortune. Ah, here they come. Stand by.

*(Enter the three **Earthmen**.)*

Frank Hullo, you funny little things! *(seeing* **Spiv***)* Good Lord, there's another one of them!

Sham Good evening. Had a good time?

Dick We've met your Bug-Eyed Monsters.

Bill And taught them how civilized beings behave.

Sham Really? And what did they say?

Frank Oh, they were tremendously impressed. They're much more intelligent than you are, of course.

Sham Are they, indeed? How nice.

Dick When we explained what life was like on Earth, they were so ashamed that they crept away.

Bill We're going to educate them. We're going to open schools all over Venus.

Sham What a good idea! But allow me to introduce a friend of mine. Earthmen, Spiv; Spiv, Earthmen.

Frank And who is this queer little fellow?

Sham Spiv's a scientist. He comes from Mercury.

Bill A scientist. How amusing!

Sham Show them your wares, Spiv.

*(***Spiv*** brings forward his suitcase and opens it, while the ***Earthmen*** regard him with amusement, as visitors to the Zoo might watch the antics of a monkey.)*

Spiv *(fishing out a piece of apparatus)* Well, gents, this is a death-ray. It'll wipe out a whole city.

*(The attitude of the ***Earthmen*** undergoes a perceptible change.)*

Frank *(taking the death-ray in his hands and examining it closely)* I say . . . this really is brilliant.

Dick *(taking death-ray in his turn)* Civilization of the highest order!

*(The **Earthmen** exchange an awkward glance.)*

Bill Er — please excuse us, sir, for being rude just now. We realize that you come from a very advanced planet.

Spiv Well, now, this *(producing another piece of apparatus)* is a disintegrator. It turns people's bodies to heaps of dust.

Frank Magnificent!

Dick How humble it makes me feel, to meet a really first-class brain!

Bill Don't interrupt. *(to **Spiv**)* Pray go on, sir.

Spiv And this *(he produces a helmet-shaped object)* is an annihilation-cap. You just put it on, think, and the whole area falls to bits.

Frank *(breathlessly)* Wonderful. Absolutely wonderful.

Bill Vastly superior to anything we've got on Earth.

Sham *(casually)* Spiv was thinking of visiting the Earth, as it happens.

Spiv Oh, no, I —

Sham Sh-h!

Frank Really? What an honour for us!

Dick All the universities will give him a degree.

Bill He'll get the Nobel Prize!

Spiv The Nobel Prize? What's that for?

Sham Peace.

Spiv *(rather bewildered)* Well, it's very kind of you gents to offer me all these honours, but the point is, will I get any money, because you see —

Frank Money? My dear sir, on my planet we honour genius. You'll make an enormous fortune.

Spiv Oh, well, in that case —

Dick You'll come with us to the Earth?

Spiv Why, yes, I'd be glad to.

Frank Splendid! What a great day for the World!

Dick Look, fellows, let's forget about the B.E.Ms. This is so much more important.

Bill But when can we start? Our space-ship's wrecked.

Spiv You can come in mine, if you like. It's quite comfortable.

Frank May we? It's so very good of you.

Dick When can we start?

Spiv Well, now, if you like.

Earthmen *(together)* Yes, let's not waste a single minute!

Gimble Aren't you going to eat your supper?

Frank Supper? We've no time for supper while genius waits. Come on, fellows, let's off to show the Earth these brilliant machines of death!

(They pick up their space-helmets.)

Bill *(bowing to **Spiv**)* You first, sir.

Spiv No, no. After you. *(He waves **Bill** forward, and turns to **Sham** as the **Earthmen** exeunt.)* Sham, old friend — I don't know how to thank you!

Sham Oh, don't mention it. It's a pleasure.

(*Exit* **Spiv**.)

Sham Well, for once, everybody's happy. But for how long, I wonder?

Gimble And they didn't even eat their supper!

Sham Well, you know what to do about that. Come on, I'm hungry.

(*They pick up the tray of food and go out as the CURTAIN falls.*)

Questions

1 Find two pieces of evidence in the play to suggest that Gimble and Sham are more intelligent than the earthmen.

2 What is there about Sham and Gimble that would make them appear comical if this play were being performed?

3 When Sham offers the earthmen a toffee, they think it may be poisoned. What does this show about the earthmen?

4 Outline three more of the less likable qualities of the earthmen.

5 Why do the B.E.Ms finally decide they don't want the earthmen?

6 Find one line that suggests that Gimble has a sense of humour.

7 What are the qualities of genius, according to the earthmen?

8 Explain the irony behind Bill's claim that Spiv will be awarded the Nobel Prize.

9 What message is the playwright trying to communicate?

10 Is this really a humorous, or a serious, play? Explain your answer.

Allan Mackay

Introduction

This is a 'costume' comedy taking an imaginative and fanciful look backwards into History as it never was but as it should have been. The rich robes of the royalty, courtiers and officials are easily manufactured from scrap pieces of material and old clothes. The armour of the knights can be put together from grey-painted cardboard or, more elaborately, from sheet tin or foil glued to cardboard. Much of the humour rests on two ingredients: the pun or play on words as demonstrated in the Executioner's role and the art of miming as seen in the chivalrous antics of Sir Blufus and Sir Angus. The latter ingredient, being visual, calls for a great deal of exaggerated movement occupying a large area of the stage. 'Punning', on the other hand, often 'passes over the heads' of the audience and the actor may need to help in communication by a judicious use of emphasis in the right places.

Cast

Chamberlain
Servant
Lord Lily
Lady Lily
Lord Fitzroy
Lady Fitzroy
King Ferd
Queen Maud
Princess Adeline
Executioner
Magician
Sir Blufus
Sir Angus
Sir Richard Trueheart
Guard
Trumpeter
Lords and ladies of the Royal Court
Servants, other guards

SCENE

The royal court of **King Ferd**, *monarch of a mythological kingdom situated nowhere in particular. Up one end, three thrones are placed on a slightly raised dais, around which the* **Chamberlain** *and* **servant** *fuss. Big doors are at the opposite end of the room. The assembled* **lords** *and* **ladies** *of the court stand around gossiping. The* **servant** *makes some remark to the* **Chamberlain**, *who is obviously irritated.*

Chamberlain   Silence, numbskull! I declare you are the lowest insect in the kingdom!

Servant   Yes, sire — in all the kingdom there's not an insect lower and that includes —

Chamberlain   Silence! You are no more use than a pair of trussed turkeyfowl!

Servant   Yes, sire — of no use at all, sire —

Chamberlain Silence! Have the King's throne pushed forward, not back. His Majesty must stand out.

Servant Yes, sire.

(*He pushes the throne forward.*)

Chamberlain And now an extra cushion for the royal seat.

Servant The very softest, sire.

(*The **servant** selects one from a pile and brings it over to the **Chamberlain**.*)

Chamberlain Ah, yes, that will do.

(*He puts it on the throne.*)

Go now and watch for the King. And mind you give me fair warning or you'll spend your old age in the dungeons. Begone, baggage!

(*The **servant** scuttles off. **Lord Lily** approaches.*)

Lord Lily Indeed, my Lord Chamberlain, you're taking a lot of trouble preparing for His Majesty's audience.

Chamberlain It is well known, Lord Lily, that the secret of the King's good humour is a comfortable throne. Only last week a squire of much promise — and top of his class in knight school — was exiled merely because the King's back ached.

Lord Lily Ah, yes, King Ferd is such a crank on physical fitness. He has passed a law against overeating at banquets until the court loses some weight.

Chamberlain I pray that His Highness will be in a good mood so that he might grant a public holiday to the castle staff next Wednesday. That's the day of the annual jousting championships on the village green.

(***Lady Lily*** *draws near with **Lord** and **Lady Fitzroy**.*)

Lady Lily I hear there are some exciting jousts to take place.

Lord Fitzroy Forsooth, the most famous knights in the realm are to take part. Personally I'm a great fan of Sir Blufus.

Lord Lily   Oddsbod! That rusty old warhorse is fit only for rescuing maidens from the clutches of evil dragons. He does nothing else, day in, day out. There's not a damsel in distress left in any part of the kingdom. Sir Blufus has rescued the lot!

Lady Lily   I have it on good report that last Thursday he was reduced to rescuing the royal cow from the royal boghole.

Lady Fitzroy   Disgraceful! I'll not wager a gold piece on him!

Lady Lily   What do you think of Sir Angus? Now there's a bold knight.

Lord Fitzroy   Tut, we can forget him. A bumbler who thinks of nothing else but slaying dragons.

Lady Lily   What is your opinion, my Lord Chamberlain?

Chamberlain   One can only judge from recent form, my Lady. It is true that Sir Blufus is sadly out of practice, what with the shortage of maidens in distress. And Sir Angus has not slain a dragon over medium size in a month.

Lord Fitzroy   Perhaps an outsider will win first prize.

Lady Fitzroy   There is much talk of a young knight on a dark horse.

Lady Lily   Ah, the new recruit from the distant Valley of the Winds — Sir Richard Trueheart.

Lady Fitzroy   What a sissy name.

Chamberlain   Sir Richard is no sissy, my Lady. In a fight, he's quite a knight.

Lady Lily   It is rumoured in court circles that today the King will select one of the knights to wear the colours of the Princess Adeline on his lance at next week's jousting.

Chamberlain   That is the subject of the coming audience.

Lady Fitzroy   Is he choosing a husband for the Princess?

Chamberlain   I believe so, my Lady. As you know, His Majesty prides courage above all other virtues, even health. So he has sent his three best knights, Angus, Blufus and Richard, on dangerous quests to the farthest reaches of the kingdom. The one who scores the highest marks in courage will wear the colours of the Princess and win her hand.

Lady Fitzroy And what of the other two? I feel so sorry for the knights when they fail to please His Majesty. The Royal Executioner is an artist with the blade. So graceful.

Lord Fitzroy With such talent he's bound to get ahead.

Lady Lily Local talk has it that he was a court jester at his last appointment. That's why he is so happy in his job.

Chamberlain Scandal, my Lady, scandal.

Lord Lily Will the executioner be here today?

Chamberlain Yes. He has had his favourite axe on the grindstone all day. And the royal carpenters have carved a new block specially inscribed with the King's family motto: Divide and Conquer.

Lady Fitzroy Jolly good show! There's nothing like an old-fashioned execution!

Lord Fitzroy And if the King is pleased, we'll all get our holiday.

*(The **servant** comes rushing in.)*

Servant The King approaches!

Chamberlain Everyone to his place! Now please remember your manners!

*(The **Chamberlain** claps his hands and the court lines up in ranks. He remains beside the throne.)*

Trumpeter, sound the salute!

*(The **trumpeter** sounds a long blast, off-key. Everyone shudders.)*

Three turns on the rack for that disgusting piece of music!

Trumpeter Mercy, sire — isn't that stretching things a bit?

Chamberlain Quiet!

*(**King Ferd** enters in style, followed by **Queen Maud, Princess Adeline**, the **Executioner** in a black mask, **two servants** carrying a block and axe and lastly the **court magician** in flowing robes covered with cryptic symbols. Everyone bows.)*

All   Hail King Ferd! Hail King Ferd!

*(During this **King Ferd** and **Queen Maud** have seated themselves on the thrones. The others stand beside the **Chamberlain**. The block and axe are placed well to the front.)*

All   Hail Queen Maud! Hail Princess Adeline!

*(**Queen** and **Princess** wave to the courtiers.)*

All   Hail royal executioner! Hail royal magician! Hail royal servants carrying the royal block —

King   Quiet! *(Dead silence.)* Our greetings to our loyal subjects. Congratulations to you, Chamberlain. First-rate show! You can have an extra ten minutes in my company as a reward.

Chamberlain   *(bowing)* Thank you, Majesty.

King   Is the room properly ventilated?

Chamberlain   Yes, sire.

King   Good. Everyone present will take three deep breaths. *(They do so.)* Splendid! *(To the **Queen**.)* Are you comfortable, my dear?

Queen   Yes, thank you Ferdie.

King   *(to **Princess**)* And you, my dear? Not sitting in a draft, are you?

Princess   Just a small one, father.

King   Chamberlain, have the door shut.

Chamberlain   Servant, shut the door!

Servant   Beg pardon, sire.

Chamberlain   Shut up!

Servant   Yes, sire. I won't say another word, never!

Chamberlain   The door, ninny!

Servant   Oh, yes.

(He runs out. There is a tremendous slam.)

Chamberlain   The door is shut, Your Highness.

*(**Servant** re-enters.)*

King   Yes, yes! Do get on with it.

Chamberlain   *(loudly)* Greetings to the all powerful King Ferd, ruler of the vast lands reaching from the Valley of the Winds in the north to the great Black Forest in the south — and perhaps beyond —

King   Perhaps, Chamberlain?

Chamberlain   Those regions are in revolt, sire. They refuse to pay taxes.

King   Did we not send an army to conquer them?

Chamberlain   Truly, sire. But the army has failed to return.

King   Why, pray?

Chamberlain   I have it on good report that it ran afoul of a particularly ferocious dragon in the neighbourhood of the Black Forest. In short, the army was eaten.

King   Egad! Armour and all?

Chamberlain   Down to the last bolt, sire.

King   One dragon for a whole army? Impossible!

Chamberlain   The winter has been very hard, sire, and the dragons are unusually hungry. One has been known to consume a whole haystack, complete with farmer and family, merely by inhaling deeply at a distance of one league.

King   Gazooks, these pests will drive me to bankruptcy! Declare a national war on dragons. Inform the minister for the army.

Chamberlain   He is no longer with us, sire.

King   Another one of his fake sick leaves, I suppose.

Chamberlain   No, sire. He was stood on by a dragon yesterday morn in Potter's Pastures.

King   Saint George and all the Saints! Didn't he have enough sense to get out of the way?

Chamberlain   It was the same dragon, sire. It has a pretty big foot.

King   *(shouting)* A fooey on its foot!

Queen   Now, Ferd, calm down or you will have a fit of the agues.

King   Yes, of course, my dear.

Queen   Whatever you do, keep your feet warm. And wrap that muffler tight around your throat or you'll catch your death.

King   Yes, dear. And now, Chamberlain, to business.

(He stands up.)

My loyal subjects!

All   Yes, Ferd.

King   *(shouting)* What?

All   Yes, King Ferd!

King   Manners, please! My loyal subjects, we are gathered to hear the accounts of three of my boldest knights who were sent early this morning on quests to prove their courage.

All   Hurrah for the knights!

King   They have recently returned and will be soon in the royal presence. The one receiving the top marks will wear the colours of Princess Adeline at next week's jousting jamboree!

All   Hurrah for the Princess!

King   This man will be her husband and your new king —

All   Hurrah for the new king!

King   When I die!

Servant   *(feebly)* Long live King Ferd!

King   *(shouting)* What?

All   *(quickly)* Long live King Ferd! Ferd forever!

King   That's better. Reward that loyal servant with first use of the royal dog's bones.

Chamberlain   It shall be done, sire.

Princess   But father, why can't I pick my own husband?

King   *(sitting)* Whatever for, child?

Princess   I want to marry the man I love.

King   Stuff and nonsense! Besides, you'll hardly ever see him. You never see a knight in the day.

Princess   But Angus and Blufus are old enough to be my fathers. They're . . . rusty!

King   By my royal beard, men my age are in the prime of life.

Princess   Couldn't I have one just approaching his prime?

King   Such as Sir Richard Trueheart?

Princess   Ah, what a romantic moonlit knight.

King   Moonlit?

Princess   He sings under my window every evening.

King   We shall see. And now, Chamberlain, before the knights arrive, the royal reports.

Chamberlain   Executioner!

Executioner   *(stepping forward)* Sire!

Chamberlain   Read the executioner's report.

*(The **executioner** bows and unfolds a scroll.)*

Executioner   Today's block tally is five: two for pickpocketing in the courtyard, two for poaching on the King's reserve, and one for writing 'Ferd is a sissy' on the castle wall.

King   The scoundrel! Paint over it, Chamberlain. Carry on, executioner.

Executioner   Three men spent the afternoon on the rack for loitering near the royal pump and one was given fifty lashes for admitting membership of the secret society for the prevention of cruelty to dragons, known in the palace underworld as S.O.L.

King   S.O.L.?

Executioner   Save Our Lizards.

King   Egad! What's the world coming to? How do you find the new block, executioner?

Executioner   Easy, sire. It's right there in front of you.

King   No, no, idiot. I mean what's it like?

Executioner   An axeman's dream, sire. Just the right height for a good swing.

King   Are you still unpopular with the people?

Executioner   In all truth, sire, they consider me as an awful pain in the neck.

King   Come, come, man — your humour is in bad taste.

Executioner   Pardon, sire — old habits die hard.

King   But not old clowns. Carry on with the reports, Chamberlain.

Chamberlain   Magician!

*(The **executioner** steps back as the **magician** takes his place, bowing gravely and unfolding his scroll.)*

Magician   Sire!

Chamberlain   Read the magician's report.

Magician   Two large spells were cast during the day: one to bring rain to the farmlands and one to rid the royal back of the agues.

King   My royal back still aches, Magician!

Magician   This spell takes two days to fall, sire.

King   Executioner!

Executioner   *(stepping up)* Yes, sire?

King   Take a note. If my back hasn't stopped aching by tomorrow night, this expensive magicman may have to invent a spell to restore his bungling head to his bungling shoulders!

Executioner   Might I say, sire, that his execution would make a wizard show.

King   And might I say that witty hatchetmen are a sovereign a dozen!

Executioner   *(stepping back)* Pardon, sire.

King   Anything further to report, faker?

Magician   One small spell was cast to make strawberries grow in the east garden.

King   I hate strawberries — they give me goosebumps.

Magician   *(sadly)* I know, sire. I planted strawberries but gooseberries came up.

King   *(furious)* And it's not raining in the farmlands, either! Begone, fool!

*(The **magician** steps back.)*

Chamberlain, let's get down to business. The knights!

All   Hurrah for the knights!

Chamberlain   Call Sir Blufus!

Guard   *(at the door)* Sir Blufus!

Princess   Father, if you make me marry this doddering old fool, I shall drink hemlock and die.

King   Hemlock? There's no hemlock in this kingdom.

Princess   Then I'll get the magician to conjure some for me.

King   Hah! You're safe.

Princess   Sir Blufus thinks of nothing but rescuing women. Why, he's already rescued me twice this week. Once, when I was caught in a storm a few yards from the palace, he came charging up on that huge plough-horse of his, picked me up and dumped me on the pommel of his saddle, then set off at a frightful rate for the castle gates. The second time I had got no further than the garden when he came leaping over the wall in full armour, threatening to draw and quarter any insect that landed on me.

King   The man is obviously devoted to you.

*(A trumpet blast is sounded, again off-key, and **Sir Blufus** enters clad in full and rusty armour. He approaches the throne and bows.)*

Welcome, Blufus.

Blufus   Thank you, sire. Is this me future bride?

Princess   Oh, horror!

King   First, Sir Blufus, your report.

*(While giving his report, **Blufus** mimes all the actions — to the danger of all.)*

Blufus   While riding the west boundaries of the kingdom, I spied this poor damsel held captive by an evil baron. She screamed for help —

King   Oh, not again.

(Everyone groans.)

Blufus, can't you find anything more exciting than damsels in distress?

Blufus   *(miming)* This was no ordinary rescue, sire. Between us lay the mighty torrent of the River Ada. Leaving me horse, I dove in and with powerful strokes swam across —

King   In full armour?

Blufus   My progress *was* rather slow, sire. For two hours I battled with the angry current until finally I arrived on the far bank.

King   Marvellous, Blufus, marvellous!

Blufus   'Twas nothing, sire.

Chamberlain Might I point out, highness, that owing to the drought mentioned by the magician, the River Ada is a mere trickle, six inches in depth.

King Are you trying to deceive us, Blufus?

Blufus Never, sire! It has since rained in that region.

King Really? Chamberlain, the magician is recalled from disgrace. Carry on, Blufus.

Blufus *(warmed up now)* Well, once on the opposite shore, I did grapple with the evil baron. All day we fought, first one having the advantage, then the other — thus!

*(His sword nearly cuts the **executioner** in two. The latter defends himself with his axe.)*

King Bravo!

All Bravo, Blufus!

Blufus In the height of the battle, I drew back and gave my war-cry: 'For Ferd and Saint George'. Upon hearing this he gave a shudder of terror and dropped his guard. I pounced like a tiger —

King Tiger, Blufus?

Blufus A beast of great speed, sire.

King Never heard of it, therefore it can't exist.

Blufus Pardon, sire — I was carried away by the memory of the contest.

King If you don't get a move on, you'll be carried away by a battalion of my guards!

Blufus Yes, sire. Well, I pounced like a rabbit — thus!

King Oh, dear.

Blufus And cleaved his pate with me sword!

King Give him full marks but take one off for making up that tale about tigers.

Chamberlain *(writing in a book)* Yes, sire.

(Everyone applauds.)

Blufus There is more, sire. I did collect the maiden from the castle, and borrowing an extra horse —

King An extra horse? The romantic way is to throw her on the pommel of your saddle.

Blufus Said maiden wouldn't . . . er . . . fit, sire, being of generous structure.

King Egad! What's her name?

Blufus 'Twas the Queen's mother.

Queen Oh, Sir Blufus, how wonderful.

King *(aghast)* Do you mean to say you spent the taxpayers' money rescuing my mother-in-law?

Blufus *(nervous)* Yes sire.

King *(standing)* Executioner!

Executioner *(stepping up eagerly)* Sire!

King Separate this idiot from his head!

Executioner A pleasure, sire.

> *(He pushes forward the block and has a couple of swings.)*

Ah, this will be a knight to remember. Come, Sir Blufus, it will teach you not to lose your head over a lady.

King Executioner! Once more and you're through!

Executioner A thousand pardons, sire. Ready, Blufus?

Blufus *(kneeling at the block)* Does this mean I don't get to wed the Princess?

King Off with his head!

Queen Ferd, stop this! After all, the lady *is* my mother.

King Impossible — she's been caught in a dragon net eight times this month — oh, very well, release him.

> *(The **executioner** is very disappointed. **Blufus** rises.)*

Queen Whom did you rescue my mother from, Sir Blufus?

Blufus   The evil Baron Bagley, m'Lady.

Queen   *(fainting)* Father!

King   Well now, that's a bit better. Chamberlain, give him average marks and impound his horse for two months.

Blufus   Mercy sire — two months! Two months without rescuing a damsel.

King   Too bad. Polish your armour. Have a bath. Dismissed.

(**Blufus** *steps back. The* **King** *tries to revive the* **Queen**.)

Feeling better, m'dear?

Queen   *(weakly)* Yes, Ferd. Alas, poor mother.

King   Buck up. I'll look after her. She can assist me in the stables.

Queen   You're very kind, Ferd.

King   It just comes naturally. Carry on, Chamberlain.

Chamberlain   Guard, call Sir Angus!

Guard   *(at door)* Sir Angus!

Princess   Oh, father, this one is worse than Blufus. Grandfather signed him on during the last Scottish wars.

King   Nonsense! There's a gallop in the old warhorse yet.

Princess   Dragons, dragons, that's all he thinks about! All day long he's out slaughtering the poor beasts to prove his love for me. And then what does he do? He cuts off their heads, props their eyes open, and lines them up on the castle wall just outside my window.

King   A lovely touch.

Princess   If you make me marry him I'll look for a witch's curse to strike me dead.

(*A trumpet blast, again off-key.* **Sir Angus** *enters, in full armour, and bows to the* **King**.)

King   A royal welcome, Sir Angus.

Angus   Begorrah, thank ye, my liege.

King   Liege? Is that one of those fancy French titles you picked up in Paris?

Angus   Aye, my liege. A bonny name, isn't it, my liege?

King   I like it — but don't overdo it.

Angus   No, sire.

King   And now, what noble deed have you performed?

Angus   Aye, a noble deed it was, sire. While patrolling the kingdom in the region of the Black Forest, I came across an extremely fierce dragon — a Dragonus Vertibrias variety.

King   Egad! The worse kind!

Blufus   A likely story. Probably a wood lizard half dead from old age.

Angus   Begorrah, be careful Blufus or I'll pin thy knightly ears back to thy knightly head!

Blufus   Pooh and piffle! I don't trifle with tellers of fairy tales!

*(**Angus** and **Blufus** are about to face up to each other.)*

Chamberlain   Gentlemen, please!

*(**Angus** calms down and turns back to the **King**. He begins to mime his story vigorously.)*

Angus In truth, ye Majesty, it was a most fearful beast, with a hundred sharp spines on its back, a spiked tail fifty yards long and a horrible river of flame at its mouth.

King Mmmmmm. That does sound a bit made-up.

Angus Oh sire, my heart is wounded.

King I don't care a royal fig about your heart. Be careful or I'll wound thy knightly rear with my royal foot.

Chamberlain Careful sire — he's still in armour.

King Oh, yes — so he is. Well, get on with it, man — there's another knight tonight.

Angus Said beast stood two hundred royal hands high, had scales as thick as the royal skull and fiery red eyes as big as the royal head.

King That's better.

(*Encouraged,* **Angus** *really puts some work into his acting.*)

Angus Upon called to battle, it gave forth with such a monstrous bellow that the very oaks in the forest shed leaves in terror. It did gnash the sod with its huge yellow fangs — as sharp as the royal wit —

King Saint George preserve us!

Angus Confronted by such a hellish sight, I drew my trusty sword 'Exchallenger' and despatched the beast with a tremendous swipe delivered from the left side — thus!

(*All applaud.*)

King Bravo, Angus! Splendid show!

Angus The head now adorns the battlements in immediate view of your bedroom window as a warning to all future dragons.

King (*nervous*) I'm not sure that's such a good idea, Angus. Did you say fiery red eyes and huge teeth?

Angus (*sadly*) I'll have the head removed, sire.

King Good. We wouldn't want to alarm the Queen, would we?

Queen There you go, Ferd, always thinking of others.

King Tush. *(To **Angus**.)* Sir Angus, I do believe you deserve top marks.

Blufus But Your Majesty, the slaying of a large dragon is no great feat these days. The kingdom abounds with such monsters and dozens are despatched each day. Why, last Tuesday, a mere farmer mortally wounded one with his pitchfork while defending his cabbage crop.

King Indeed! Sir Angus, you have been leading me up the royal garden path. Perhaps you need a turn or two on the new rack I recently imported from France.

Angus Mercy, Sire.

King Ah, a beautiful job! It has fifteen more notches than the old German type and gives a much more delicate touch. Is that not so, executioner?

Executioner You may say, sire, that you are not stretching the truth.

King Chamberlain, reward Sir Angus with an hour on the rack and take five sovereigns from the executioner's pay packet for trying to be funnier than his king.

Angus But, Your Majesty, my dragon was much more than just big and ferocious.

King Indeed?

Angus Truly sire. Upon seeing my face, the creature uttered a series of insulting remarks against thy royal self.

King Monstrous! What did it say?

Angus It said it would singe your beard with its flame and . . .

King Go on, man, go on!

Angus It said only billy goats had beards. Then it snickered and made a very rude sound with its lips.

King What sound?

Angus I believe, sire, the villagers call it the royal raspberry.

(He demonstrates.)

King   A beast of the devil!

Angus   Well, upon hearing that, I saw red —

King   Saw red, Angus?

Angus   That was the colour of the dragon, sire.

Blufus   Ha! Dragons can't talk and everyone knows that they're not red. They're black with green spots.

Angus   Are you calling me a liar, Blufus?

Blufus   Sir Angus had so much whiskey last night, he probably thought his horse talked to him too!

Angus   Begorrah! More insults to the noble house of Angus. Have at you, Blufus!

*(Both men draw swords and begin to fight in an exaggerated fashion. Everyone enjoys it hugely. Finally, with a mighty swipe, **Blufus** sends **Angus** backwards into the **King**. **Ferd** disappears under a pile of armour. Everyone, except **Ferd**, cheers.)*

King   *(struggling up)* Executioner!

Executioner   Sire!

King   Despatch that clumsy dolt immediately!

Executioner   Yes, sire!

*(He drags **Angus** over to the block, singing loudly.)*

Oh, how these knights do drag on!

King   That does it! Executioner, turn in your axe!

Executioner   Forgive me, sire — it slipped out.

King   If it's one thing I can't stand it's a funny axeman! It's downright improper.

Chamberlain   Might I remind the King that skilled executioners are in short supply at the moment. There are not enough prisoners for an apprentice to practise on.

King   What a terrible state of affairs. Very well, executioner, one last chance. Angus, report to the rack. You could do with a few more inches on you.

Angus *(stepping back)* Thank you, sire.

Queen You're too soft, Ferd.

King It is kingly to forgive, my dear. *(To **Chamberlain**.)* Have the last knight in.

Chamberlain Call Sir Richard!

Guard *(at door)* Sir Richard!

Princess Oh father, let this one win, please!

*(**Sir Richard** enters, bright and shiny. He bows.)*

King We welcome our new recruit, Sir Richard.

Richard Greetings, Majesty. Hello Addy, my love.

King Addy? Good grief, this is a royal courtroom, not a park bench!

Richard My apologies, sire. I was carried away by the princess's beauty — which I see she inherits from her father.

King Ahem — granted. But please address her in the proper manner in future. And now, what have you been up to today?

Richard Not much, sire. I spent most of it with the Princess.

*(**Princess** giggles.)*

King Strange. I ordered you to go questing alone.

Richard What a bore. I spent my hours in your rose garden playing and singing to the Princess on my lute.

Princess Oh, Richard, my nightingale.

Richard Addy, my sweet little rose.

King Executioner!

Executioner Sire!

King In all my born years, I never heard such rubbish. Off with his head!

Princess Father, spare him or I shall throw myself off the battlements!

King   Hemlock, witch's curses, high jumping! My head is going round in circles.

Queen   Now, Ferd, remember your ague.

King   A royal fooey on my ague! Carry on!

Princess   Please father . . .

King   *(shouting)* Divide and conquer!

    *(The **executioner** grabs **Richard** and puts his head on the block. He struggles.)*

Executioner   Hold still, you blockhead.

King   Executioner!

Executioner   Oh, no — I've done it again, haven't I?

King   Yes you have! Draw your pay! You're through and that's final!

Executioner   Sire, I deserve it all. But let me have one last chop for the road.

King   Very well. Make it quick.

Richard   Majesty, may I have one last word?

King   What is it?

Richard   You ordered us to perform the deed of greatest courage possible to mankind. Is that not so?

King   Yes.

Richard   I have performed that deed.

King   You have?

Richard   Of course! I have disobeyed your order. Doesn't that take a terrific amount of courage?

King   *(thinking)* So it does, Sir Richard, arise! To defy the King is to defy death itself. I award you top marks, the title of prince and my daughter's hand in marriage.

All   Hurrah for Prince Richard!

Princess Oh, father, I am so happy.

*(She goes to **Richard**.)*

King And now, I declare a public holiday with full pay to all members of the castle staff next Wednesday!

All Hurrah for Ferd!

King What?

All Hurrah for Ferd the King!

King That's better. Court dismissed.

*(All go gaily, except **Ferd**. Once alone, he goes over, picks up the executioner's axe, and stands up on the block.)*

King Well, Ferd, what a splendid, healthy king you are!

*(The **Chamberlain** rushes in.)*

Chamberlain Sire, sire! There are posters up all over the castle walls.

King What do they say, man?

Chamberlain Ahem. 'Ferd is a big fat failure.'

King *(shouting)* Executioner!

*(The **executioner** rushes in.)*

Executioner Yes, sire?

King Find the villain who painted those posters! Have you read them?

Executioner Oh, yes, sire. 'Ferd is a big fat failure.' Shocking!

King Disgusting!

Executioner Insulting! Fancy not addressing you as King Ferd —

King Executioner!

*(**King Ferd** comes bounding down off the block, brandishing the axe. The **executioner** and **Chamberlain** turn and flee, chased by the **King**.)*

CURTAIN

Questions

1 Explain how the servant usually responds to reprimands by the Chamberlain.

2 Comment on the language used in the line describing the executioner: 'With such talent he's bound to get ahead'.

3 Why does Ferd become upset from time to time with his loyal subjects?

4 What is there about the royal executioner that frequently angers the king?

5 Explain how Sir Blufus's story earns a reprieve for the magician.

6 Who is the evil Baron Bagley?

7 What three ways of ending her life does Princess Adeline threaten to use?

8 What insulting things did Sir Angus's dragon say and do?

9 Why does Blufus think Angus is lying?

10 In what way is the new French rack an improvement on the older German one?

11 Explain how Sir Richard Trueheart has performed the bravest deed.

12 Explain how the royal executioner misses the point of the king's objections to the signs, 'Ferd is a big fat failure'. Why do the signs upset the king? Why does the executioner think the king is upset?

Hijack

Charles Wells

Cast

Professor Manningtree	A professor of history
Wing-Commander Fanshaw	Ex-RAF (very)
Enid Fanshaw	His unobtrusive wife
Travers..	A somewhat aggressive businessman
Miss Madeleine Pringle	An elderly lady making her first flight
Peter **Steve** **Graham**	Schoolboys and classmates
Captain Stewart	The pilot (heard over the loudspeaker)
Shafti **Mustapha**	Hijackers of a 'Middle-Eastern' appearance
Janet Davidson	The stewardess
1st Chess Player	
2nd Chess Player	
Other Passengers	

Captain Stewart's voice over the loudspeaker Ladies and gentlemen, this is Captain Stewart speaking. We are now over the Atlantic Ocean and flying at 30 000 feet. The weather in New York is warm and sunny. Seventy-eight degrees to be exact. Flying conditions are perfect and we may well arrive a few minutes early.

(The loudspeaker clicks off.)

*(A swarthy passenger, **Mustapha**, who has been sitting inconspicuously near the back of the plane, walks down the gangway and through the doorway marked 'Crew Only' leading to the pilot's cabin. The **stewardess** hurries down the gangway after him.)*

Miss Davidson *(shouting)* Excuse me, sir, you're going the wrong way. You're not allowed in there!

*(Before she can pursue him through the doorway **Shafti** springs to his feet, brandishing a large pistol.)*

Shafti Stop! I am holding a gun! Sit down please. Ladies and gentlemen, this airplane has been seized in the name of the People's Republic of El Shiraz. Please not to panic. Remain in your sittings and nobody will be damaged.

(There is a moment of stunned silence. Then everybody starts to speak at once. Through the hubbub the following remarks can be heard.)

Travers This is outrageous! This is a *British* plane, sir!

Fanshaw Look here old man. There are women and children on board y'know. *(to his wife)* Steady on, Enid old girl.

Mrs Fanshaw *(continuing to knit)* Yes dear.

Steve This is fantastic!

Peter What a story to tell them back at school.

Graham Just like this film I saw. 'Sky Pirates' it was called. There was this bloke who . . .

Peter and **Steve** *(in unison)* We've *seen* it!

Miss Pringle *(to **Fanshaw**)* Excuse me. I do beg your pardon but this is so new to me. There's a gentleman standing over there and he's holding something in his hand that looks awfully like a pistol. We haven't got to New York yet have we? My sister Millicent says that everyone in America carries a pistol. She has a television, you see. I know it's supposed to take three-quarters of an hour but the captain did say we might be early, didn't he? Has the plane stopped?

1st Chess Player   Checkmate.

Shafti   What is that you are saying?

Professor   *(helpfully)* He said 'checkmate'.

Shafti   Why are you calling me 'mate'? My country and yours are enemies. I am not your mate. Fifteen of my countrymen are in British prisons. That is why we have overtaken your plane. We will not let you go until our brave freedom fighters are back on Shirazi dirt.

Professor   *(helpful still)* Soil.

Shafti   Thank you. Yes. Soil. *(He is standing at one end of the gangway and watching the passengers warily, gun waving menacingly from side to side.)*

Travers   But dammit man, this plane will be in New York in five hours' time, so how can . . .

Shafti   *(interrupting)* Oh no, my English mate. In less than five hours this plane will be in El Shiraz.

Travers   This is preposterous. I have a very important business conference this afternoon. I absolutely refuse to go to . . . to . . .

Professor   *(helpfully again)* El Shiraz.

Travers   We refuse, I tell you.

Shafti   But I am pointing the gun. I am holding — how do you say it? — all the trumpets.

Professor   Trumps.

Shafti   Thank you. Yes. Trumps.

Captain Stewart's voice over the loudspeaker   Ladies and gentlemen. This is Captain Stewart speaking. May I have your attention please. As you must be aware by now, a most regrettable incident has occurred. However, I can assure you that

there is absolutely no cause for alarm. I want all of you to do exactly as Mr Shafti says. On no account is anybody to attempt to disarm him. Such an action could conceivably jeopardise the safety of us all. I'm afraid I have no option but to obey Mr Mustapha, who is here in the cockpit with me now, and to turn the plane and head back in the direction from which we have come. It goes without saying that I deeply regret having to take such action, but I can assure you that I am left with no alternative. Please co-operate with Mr Shafti as far as is reasonably possible. Remember there is absolutely no danger so long as you do so. I will give you further information in due course. Thank you.

(The loudspeaker clicks off.)

Fanshaw This is disgraceful. Stewart's an ex-RAF chap. Bomber Command. Got no right to give such an order. Duty of every officer to try to escape when in the hands of the enemy. When I was a prisoner of war back in . . .

Miss Davidson   Ladies and gentlemen. With Mr Shafti's permission, and bearing in mind what the Captain has just said, I will be coming round with coffee and sandwiches in a few minutes.

Travers   Make mine a double whisky and soda.

Fanshaw   Think I'll join you old boy.

Shafti   No, you must stay where you are please. All except the waitress must remain in his seats.

Steve   Have you got an atlas in your bag, Graham?

Graham   I think so, why?

Steve   I want to see where this El Shiraz place is.

Graham   *(finding atlas)* Sounds like the Middle-East. Yes, here it is. Page 16.

Peter   *(looking over his shoulder and pointing)* Look. There it is. On the Red Sea.

Steve   Not very big, is it?

Graham   Hardly big enough for an airfield by the look of it.

Peter   Well, we'll have to come down *somewhere*, that's for sure.

Steve   Unless all the engines fail and we're stuck up here.

(The other two boys laugh at this. As the laughter dies down we hear . . .)

Miss Pringle   You know, Wing-Commander, this gets more and more puzzling. The captain said we were turning round, didn't he? Well, when we get back to London what time will it be? Will it be the day *after* tomorrow? You see, my sister Millicent visits her niece in Hampshire on Fridays and I have to feed the cat. He's a blue Persian, you know.

Fanshaw   Sounds like Mr Shafti — though come to think of it I should imagine he's more of a *red* Persian, what? *(He chuckles at his own cleverness.)*

Professor   *(who does not share **Fanshaw's** sense of humour)* Actually, Wing-Commander, Persia's over a thousand miles from El Shiraz.

Travers   These countries are all the same. No respect for the Union Jack any more, any of them. Pity we closed down our bases over there. A couple of infantry battalions would soon stop their little game.

Fanshaw   Infantry? No, a fighter squadron would do the trick in half the time. These foreign chappies soon take to their heels when a couple of dozen Phantoms open up on them. I remember one afternoon near Tobruk . . .

*(His voices fades into the background and we hear those of the two **chess players**, who have been quietly getting on with their game, oblivious, apparently, of the events of the preceding few minutes.)*

1st Chess Player   A good move. You have my rook. By the way, wasn't that the captain's voice over the loudspeaker just now?

2nd Chess Player   Was it? I heard nothing.

1st Chess Player   Well it can't have been anything important. Now it's my move I believe. How can I escape?

Shafti   *(Jerking to attention at the word 'escape'. His concentration has been wandering a little. Standing pointing a gun can soon get tiring.)* What are you saying? Escape? There shall be no escaping. You will all remain in our fingers until the British Government releases my fellow countrymen.

Professor   Didn't you people hijack a Swiss plane a few weeks ago?

Shafti   Yes. The passengers are now in goal in Shiraz.

Graham   You mean they're *playing football* out there?

Professor   I think Mr Shafti means they're in *gaol*.

Shafti   Gaol. Yes, that is the word. And they are staying there until the Swiss Government pays us back the money it has stolen from us.

Professor   How did the Swiss come to steal money from you?

Shafti   For many years my country has been ruled by Sheikh Suleiman. But last year we were revolting . . .

Fanshaw   *(aside to* **Travers***)* You're still pretty repulsive *this* year if you ask me.

Shafti   . . . and Sheikh Suleiman was shot. When we tried to get back all the money he had gathered — money that belongs to the people of Shiraz — we found that he had put it in a bank in Switzerland. The Swiss Government refuses to repay it. So we blow up their plane and lock up their passengers. And now we wait.

Travers   And what, may I ask, do you propose to do with *us* if we ever reach your country?

Shafti   You will be locked up too. Until your Government releases the fifteen Shirazi liberation fighters that are in your prisons.

Travers   And what were they put in prison *for*?

Shafti   They have been blowing up oil pipelines over the border in Quatan, which is still a British colony.

Fanshaw   I'm glad to hear we've still got one left. The last government must have forgotten all about that one.

Miss Davidson   *(as she distributes drinks)* But surely, Mr Shafti, if these men went round deliberately blowing up pipelines in another country they can hardly complain about being punished.

Shafti   *(warming to his theme)* But you see, the pipe was carrying away *our* oil — oil belonging to the people of El Shiraz. It was carrying it to the sea to be shipped off by a British company.

Travers   But dammit man, the company was paying you for the oil, wasn't it?

Shafti *(triumphantly)* Ah, but you see the money was going not to the Shirazi people but into the Swiss bank of Sheikh Suleiman.

Professor Which is where we came in, I think.

Miss Pringle Yes, that's right. This is the door we came in by. I remember distinctly. Are we supposed to go out by the same door? *(She stands up.)* I must hurry back to my sister's and feed the cat.

Shafti Please be sitting down madam.

Miss Pringle I beg your pardon, young man, but I am most anxious to get off the plane as soon as possible. Have the stairs been put in position yet? *(She looks about her in confusion.)*

Fanshaw I'm afraid they'll need to be pretty long ones, we're still at 30 000 feet.

Miss Pringle I thought we were back in London. Really, this is all *most* confusing.

Professor *(gently)* I'm afraid this is going to come as rather a shock to you. Will you listen very carefully? This plane is now on its way to El Shiraz, a small country on the Red Sea.

Miss Pringle But this is British Airways flight 702 to New York. I was *most* careful to get on the right plane. I remember once catching what I thought was the Manchester train and arriving in Plymouth. You see, I was there at the right time and I was on the right platform, but I'd gone to Paddington instead of Euston. Ever since then I've been *so* careful.

Professor Yes, this *is* the New York plane — or at least it *was.* *(A look of total non-comprehension suffuses* **Miss Pringle's** *face.)* I'm afraid we've been hijacked. That young man with the gun in his hand has made the pilot turn the plane round and take us to El Shiraz.

Miss Pringle You know, I *thought* that was a gun, but I've got my *reading* glasses on, you see, and I wasn't quite sure. I'm afraid I've always had rather poor eyesight. The other day I was in the bank writing a . . .

1st Chess Player Check!

Miss Pringle *(puzzled)* No, actually I think it was a paying-in form, but it doesn't really affect the story . . . (**Miss Davidson** *puts an end to anecdote with a cup of coffee.*)

Captain Stewart's voice over the loudspeaker Ladies and gentlemen, this is Captain Stewart. May I have your attention, please. We are now over the Mediterranean, and I anticipate landing at the Shiraz airstrip in about three-quarters of an hour. I will then be permitted to make radio contact with London to arrange for your relatives to be informed of the situation. Will you please write down the names, addresses and, where possible, the 'phone numbers of those you wish to be notified. The stewardess will collect them. Let me reassure you that there is no cause for alarm. The airstrip at Shiraz is perfectly adequate for this type of aircraft, and though the landing may be a trifle bumpier than at Heathrow you may rest assured that it will be perfectly normal. Once we are down we will be in the hands of the . . . er . . . Shirazi Revolutionary Council who will be in constant touch with the Government in London. I'm sure it will not be long before we are permitted to leave. Thank you. *(The loudspeaker clicks off.)*

Professor He's whistling to keep our spirits up. I can't see them letting us go in a hurry.

Fanshaw Those Swissair passengers have been held prisoner for over a month, haven't they?

Professor Yes, I believe so.

Shafti *(brandishing his pistol)* You have all heard what your captain has said. In a few minutes now you will be in the People's Republic of El Shiraz. You will be well looked at there.

Professor Looked *after*.

Shafti Thank you. Yes. Looked *after*.

Fanshaw *(quietly)* Probably well looked *at* as well. I know these chappies. Met 'em in the war. Sight of an Englishman they all come crowding round staring and trying to sell you postcards.

Travers They won't get much change out of me, I can tell you. *(He pauses.)* Wait a minute. Do they wear shoes, these native fellows?

Fanshaw I dare say some of them own the odd sandal or two, why?

Travers *(brightening)* Might be a chance for me to do a business deal after all. I say . . . er . . . Mr Shafti . . .

Shafti *(approaching suspiciously)* What are you wanting?

Travers I wondered whether your . . . *(He hesitates, then pronounces the next word with some difficulty.)* . . . government might be interested in a large consignment of shoes I happen to have available. Best quality leather, complete range of sizes. Could arrange to have them shipped out to your place . . .

Shafti Shoes? *(as though reciting from a pamphlet)* The people of my country in their heroic struggle against the forces of imperialism have no need of *shoes*. Shoes to us are a symbol of the decadence of Western society. *(In a different tone.)* Now if it is a question of *guns* . . .

Travers *(hesitantly at first)* Well . . . a friend of mine in Birmingham does a nice little line in machine-pistols. I think it's possible that . . .

Shafti *(beaming)* Ah! Now we are — how do you say it? — cooking with oil.

Professor Gas. Tell me, Mr Shafti, have you lived in England? You seem, if I may say so, to have a remarkable grasp of our language and its idiom.

Shafti *(pleased)* Oh yes! I was for two years at your London School of Economics.

Fanshaw *(aside)* At *our* expense, no doubt! Fine thing when the British tax-payer pays out good money to train you foreign chappies to steal our oil and hijack our planes . . .

Professor *(who has heard the remark, though **Shafti** appears not to have done)* I don't think even the London School of Economics runs a degree course in hijacking yet, Wing-Commander. I know one can take a degree in most subjects these days . . .

Travers *(in a markedly more friendly manner)* Tell me, how did you enjoy your two years in London, Mr Shafti?

Shafti *(relaxing now)* London is a fine city, that I am not denying, but your English winter, it seems to last for eleven months. In my bed-sitting-room in Hackney was this very little fire with this very enormous appetite for ten-penny pieces. That fire was better fed than I was. What my landlady cooked for me I would not give to my uncle's camel — and the camel is eating almost anything I am telling you. But so many fine buildings and statues there are in London. Especially I like Napoleon's Column in Trafalgar Square, and that statue of one of your kings outside the Parliament — Richard the Cowardly Lion I believe I heard someone call him, though he is looking brave enough to me, waving his scimitar in the sky up there on his horse. And your underground! It is more quickly by pipe as you Londoners say — like our oil, is it not so? In my country the girls show only their eyes, but in London . . .

Travers   *(interrupting)* This friend of mine in Birmingham, Mr Shafti, that I was telling you about. Remarkably decent fellow he is, actually. Owes me a favour as a matter of fact. I think I could persuade him to let you have a few crates of those machine-pistols for only . . . well, if I twist his arm, let's say . . . *(He and Shafti converse quietly to one side.)*

Fanshaw   *(making conversation)* Well, we won't forget this trip in a hurry, Professor.

(Travers and Shafti pass down the gangway out of earshot, deep in conversation.)

Professor   Good lord, Wing-Commander, I think you may have given me an idea. *(to Mrs Fanshaw)* May I ask what you're knitting, Mrs Fanshaw?

Mrs Fanshaw   *(surprised)* A balaclava helmet for Cyril — he feels the cold so in his ears poor thing, don't you dear?

Fanshaw   *(not pleased)* So you keep telling me, my dear.

Professor   May I borrow the ball of wool for a moment? *(He takes it and examines it closely to the bewilderment of the Fanshaws.)* Good thick stuff, this. *(Almost to himself.)* If one were to twist two or three strands together it would be pretty strong . . . in fact strong enough not to break if someone were to run into it.

Fanshaw   I say, old man, I think I'm beginning to see what you're driving at.

Professor   If we could tie it across the gangway at about ankle height and pull it nice and taut, then anyone coming along at anything above a slow walk would be almost bound to go flat on his face.

Fanshaw He'd never see it at that height, especially this dark grey colour. We just have to wait until he's not looking and then rig it up quickly.

Professor It's not quite as simple as that. We have to find some way of getting him up here at a brisk pace. We can't afford to bungle it a second time, we'll be touching down soon .

Travers *(who has just rejoined them, **Shafti** having remained at the further end of the gangway)* What's all this?

Fanshaw I've had another idea.

Professor We're going to fix a trip wire — a trip *wool* actually — for your friend Mr Shafti. If he takes a tumble over this he's bound to let go of the gun. Once we've got that we must have a good chance of dealing with his friend before we land in Shiraz.

Fanshaw *(to his wife)* Twist together some wool, Enid, treble thickness. We'll need some to tie him up with as well. *(**Mrs Fanshaw** busies herself with the wool.)*

Travers Wait a minute. Aren't we taking a bit of a risk? I mean supposing the gun goes off? He doesn't seem a bad sort of a fellow when you get to know him a bit. I think the best thing to do is to wait until we land, and then . . .

Professor I thought you had an urgent appointment in New York?

Travers Yes, well I . . . er . . . I mean I'm just thinking of the safety of the passengers, you understand. I'm sure that once we are in Shiraz we could do some kind of a deal with . . . *(He tails off under withering looks from the **Professor** and **Fanshaw**.)*

Fanshaw Quick, while Shafti's looking the other way.

Captain Stewart's voice over the loudspeaker *(While he speaks **Fanshaw** and the **Professor** tie the wool across the gangway.)* Ladies and gentlemen, this is Captain Stewart speaking. If you look down to your right you can see the Red Sea and the Arabian coast. We should be over El Shiraz in about fifteen minutes. *(The loudspeaker clicks off.)*

Fanshaw   Fifteen minutes. No time to lose. We must find a way to get Shafti up to this end — and at the double.

Professor   Leave that to me. I'll make a move for the cockpit door. He's bound to rush up here to stop me.

Travers   Supposing he shoots?

Professor   That's a chance I'll have to take — but I'm pretty sure he won't. You two get ready to grab his gun and tie him up. Better gag him too. Ready?

Travers   *(reluctantly)* OK.

Fanshaw   Roger.

(**Professor Manningtree** *stands up and makes for the door leading to the pilot's cabin.*)

Shafti   Hey! Stop! Go back to your sitting. Stop, I am saying, or I will fire you!

(**Professor Manningtree** *takes no notice. Brandishing his pistol and continuing to shout,* **Shafti** *hurries up the gangway towards him and falls headlong over the tautly-stretched wool, giving a strangled cry as he does so. The gun flies out of his hand and vanishes.* **Fanshaw** *and* **Travers** *leap on him. The* **Professor** *spins round and helps them to overpower* **Shafti***, tie and gag him, and bundle him, still struggling violently, into a pair of empty seats so that he is out of sight from the front of the plane. A cheer goes up from the rest of the* **passengers***, several of whom have by now rendered assistance.*)

Fanshaw   *(breathless)* It worked!

Professor   Yes. I hope he enjoyed his trip! *(General laughter.)*

Mrs Fanshaw   *(looking up from her knitting)* Well *done*, Professor!

Steve   Great stuff!

Peter   Put up a good fight, though, didn't he?

Graham   Just like Alan Ladd in 'Shane'.

(*Expressions of approval and congratulation are heard from various other passengers, several of whom crowd round the* **Professor***, pat him on the back, shake his hand, and so on. While this is going on the cockpit door flies open and* **Mustapha** *appears, gun in hand, and extremely agitated.*)

Mustapha   (*shouting above the din*) Back in your seats, all of you! Move! (*Reluctantly those **passengers** who are on their feet do as he says.*) What is going on? Where is Shafti?

Professor   (*aside*) I'm afraid he's a bit tied up at the moment.

Mustapha   Who has the gun? (*There is a long pause. Nobody speaks. Everyone looks at everyone else. **Mustapha** glares at each in turn, brandishing his pistol wildly.*) I am ordering you to speak! Release my friend! Hand over the gun! You cannot get away from this!

Professor   (*helpfully*) With this.

Mustapha   (*automatically*) Yes, *with* this. (*fiercely*) I am warning you. I shall shoot.

(*He walks slowly down the gangway, looking from side to side, gun waving menacingly in his fist. Eventually he sees **Shafti** still lying trussed up across two seats. He speaks to him briefly in his own language. **Shafti** grunts through his gag.*)

Untie him!

(*This to the three boys, who are nearby. They hesitate.*)

Untie him I say to you.

(He points the gun at them. Slowly and reluctantly they begin to do as he says, but stop as soon as **Mustapha** *turns back to face the rest of the passengers.)*

One of you has the gun. Let me have it! In five minutes we shall be in the glorious People's Republic of El Shiraz. I *order* you to hand over the gun.

Miss Pringle Is this what you are looking for, young man? *(She stands up and holds out* **Shafti's** *pistol at arm's length, looking at it distastefully.)*

Mustapha *(relieved, and calmer now)* Yes. Throw it on the floor please.

Miss Pringle Young man, I am not in the habit of throwing things.

Mustapha *(momentarily nonplussed)* But I am telling you to let me have this gun! *(He waves his own gun threateningly.)*

Miss Pringle *(icily)* I should be grateful if you would refrain from pointing that nasty pistol in my direction. I have a nephew of about your age, and if he were to behave in this disgraceful way I can assure you that I would cut him out of my will immediately. I think, young man, it would be better for all concerned if *you* were to hand over *your* gun to *me*. I feel sure I am speaking for *all* the passengers when I say that we have no wish to go to Algiers across your date-line. As a matter of fact I don't eat dates myself. I've always been given to understand that they are bad for one's teeth. And it is most important to me that today is the eighteenth and not the nineteenth. I've knitted this mauve pullover, you see.

(*Mustapha* clearly does not *see. He looks thoroughly confused by this speech, not without reason. He stands uncertainly in the gangway, still pointing the gun in* **Miss Pringle's** *direction, but obviously baffled as to what to do next. The rest of the passengers, thoroughly absorbed by this confrontation, look intently from one to the other. The three boys have completely abandoned any pretence of untying* **Shafti**, *who remains as he was. There is a tense silence.*)

Mustapha (*almost desperately*) You do not seem to understand. You are prisoners of the People's Republic of El Shiraz.

Miss Pringle Nonsense. We are on our way to New York. Indeed we should have been there by now were it not for this outrageous episode. I think you have delayed us long enough. You have behaved abominably, but if you hand over your pistol we will try to say no more about the matter.

(*Mustapha* mutters something in his own language. It does not sound complimentary. He makes a move towards* **Miss Pringle**.)

Stop where you are. 'Put your hands above your head' I believe is the expression one uses on such occasions. You see, my sister Millicent has a television set.

(*Mustapha* stops, uncertainly, and casts a swift and somewhat bewildered glance about the plane, almost as if seeking support from the other passengers. Nobody speaks. Nobody moves. The only sound is a muffled grunt from the gagged* **Shafti**, *now completely forgotten.*)

Mustapha (*angrily*) Drop the gun or I fire!

Miss Pringle How dare you threaten me! I always understood that you Oriental people had a reputation for courtesy and good manners.

(*Mustapha* makes a sudden rush towards* **Miss Pringle**, *clearly intent upon seizing the gun by force. There is a loud bang and* **Mustapha** *reels back, clutching his arm. His face exhibits astonishment as much as pain. His gun* *clatters to the floor and* **Professor Manningtree** *retrieves it. Delight and surprise in equal measure are to be seen on the faces of the passengers — save that of* **Miss Pringle**, *who remains calm and dignified.*)

Miss Pringle   Young man, I warned you to keep your distance. Now you must face the consequences of your reprehensible behaviour.

(**Professor Manningtree** *and* **Fanshaw** *step forward and seize* **Mustapha**, *who has gone down on one knee and is looking ruefully at his injured arm. He offers no resistance as they lead him to an empty seat where other passengers stand guard over him.*)

Wing-Commander, perhaps you would care to take possession of this unpleasant object.

(**Fanshaw** *takes the pistol from her and pockets it.* **Miss Davidson** *hurries along the gangway and through the doorway to the pilot's cabin just as the loudspeaker clicks on and we hear . . .*)

Captain Stewart's voice over the loudspeaker   This is Captain Stewart speaking. Will you please fasten your seatbelts and extinguish all cigarettes. We are making our approach to the El Shiraz airstrip and we should touch down in . . .

(*He breaks off and a muttered conversation between himself and* **Miss Davidson** *can be partly heard — words such as 'gun', 'injured', 'overpowered', and 'safe' may be picked out. He resumes his speech to the passengers.*)

Ladies and gentlemen, you seem to have the advantage over me. I have just been informed that the plane is now safely back in British hands. I would like to thank those involved in this dramatic rescue, especially the gallant lady who, I understand, disarmed the fellow who has been poking the barrel of his gun into my left ear for most of the journey. I am now turning the plane and heading back towards the Mediterranean. We will stop for refuelling at Gibraltar and should reach New York in approximately eight hours from now. Thank you.

Fanshaw   Dashed fine show, Miss Pringle!

Graham   Yes, jolly well done.

Professor   A splendid performance.

Travers Just what I've always said. No moral fibre, these foreign fellows. Your Englishman will always come out best in the end.

Mrs Fanshaw *(pointedly, continuing to knit)* Or your English *woman*.

Travers Oh, . . . er quite so, quite so.

Professor *(rather coldly)* Pity about your friend in Birmingham, though, eh?

Travers Birmingham? Oh, . . . er . . . just humouring the fellow, of course. No point upsetting him you know. Thoroughly bad piece of work, obviously. *(He looks at his watch.)* Think I should just about make that business conference in New York after all.

Miss Pringle Excuse me, Wing-Commander, but will it be a *Thursday* in Gibraltar? And will I have to fasten my safety-belt again? I do find all this so confusing.

Fanshaw *(sitting beside her and settling himself for a lengthy session)* Well now, Miss Pringle . . . *(The rest of the conversation is lost.)*

Graham Won't they be jealous back at school when they hear all about this!

Peter Not half! Reminds me of a film I once saw. What was it called, Steve? *(He nudges him and winks.)*

Steve   Oh yes. I know the one you mean. Percy Bloggs in 'Son of Batman Strikes Again'.

Graham   *(earnestly)* Hey, I don't think I've seen that one! *(**Steve** and **Peter** erupt in laughter.)*

Travers   *(with another glance at his watch)* Stewardess! *(**Miss Davidson** comes up.)* Drinks all round called for, I think. *(to **Professor Manningtree**)* Looks as though I'll sell those shoes after all!

1st Chess Player   *(who, like his friend, has remained quietly in his seat throughout the flight)* Checkmate! *(The neighbouring passengers have moved away towards the free drinks, leaving the **Chess Players** by themselves.)* Well, do we wait until the plane has left Gibraltar?

2nd Chess Player   Yes, then we stick to Gonzales's original plan. I take the pilot, you see to the passengers.

1st Chess Player   *(looking at his watch)* We should reach Cuba by nine.

2nd Chess Player   Right, comrade. Pawn to Queen 4. Your move.

*(As the rest of the passengers noisily celebrate their escape the two **Chess Players** quietly resume their game.)*

CURTAIN

Questions

1 How can you tell from Shafti's words that he is not an Englishman?

2 In what ways is Captain Stewart a typical pilot?

3 At the beginning, how do Steve, Peter and Graham react to Shafti's hijacking of the plane?

4 What reason does Shafti give for the hijack?

5 Do you think *Hijack* is a humorous play in some ways? Why?

6 Describe a part of the play where there is a great deal of tension and suspense.

7 Do you like Travers? Why?

8 What comments would you make about the character of Mustapha?

9 Did you expect Miss Pringle to shoot Mustapha? Why?

10 Do you feel that the very ending of the play has a feeling of suspense? Why?

Cast

Mrs Stevenson
First Operator
First Man
Second Man
Chief Operator
Second Operator
Third Operator
Fourth Operator
Fifth Operator
Information
Hotel Receptionist
Western Union Man
Sergeant Duffy

Lucille Fletcher

Sorry Wrong Number

A number is being dialled on a phone. Busy signal.

Mrs Stevenson *(a querulous, self-centred neurotic)* Oh — dear!

> *(Slams down receiver. Dials* **Operator**.*)*

First Operator Your call, please?

Mrs Stevenson Operator? I've been dialling Murray Hill 4-0098 now for the last three-quarters of an hour, and the line is always busy. But I don't see how it *could* be busy that long. Will you try it for me, please?

First Operator Murray Hill 4-0098? One moment please.

Mrs Stevenson I don't see how it could be busy all this time. It's my husband's office. He's working late tonight, and I'm all alone here in the house. My health is very poor — and I've been feeling so nervous all day . . .

First Operator Ringing Murray Hill 4-0098 . . .

> *(Phone buzz. It rings three times. Receiver is picked up at the other end.)*

First Man Hello.

Mrs Stevenson Hello . . . ? *(A little puzzled.)* Hello. Is Mr Stevenson there?

First Man *(into phone, as though he had not heard)* Hello . . . *(Louder)* Hello.

Second Man *(slow heavy quality, faintly foreign accent)* Hello.

First Man Hello. George?

Second Man Yes, sir.

Mrs Stevenson *(louder and more imperious, to phone)* Hello. Who's this? What number am I calling, please?

First Man We have heard from our client. He says the coast is clear for tonight.

Second Man Yes, sir.

First Man Where are you now?

Second Man In a phone booth.

First Man Okay. You know the address. At eleven o'clock the private

patrolman goes around to the bar on Second Avenue for a beer. Be sure that all the lights downstairs are out. There should be only one light visible from the street. At eleven-fifteen a subway train crosses the bridge. It makes a noise — in case her window is open, and she should scream.

Mrs Stevenson   *(shocked)* Oh — HELLO! What number is this, please?

Second Man   Okay, I understand.

First Man   Make it quick. As little blood as possible. Our client does not wish to make her suffer long.

Second Man   A knife okay, sir?

First Man   Yes. A knife will be okay. And remember — remove the rings and bracelets, and the jewellery in the bureau drawer. Our client wishes it to look like simple robbery.

Second Man   Okay — I get —

   (A bland buzzing signal.)

Mrs Stevenson   *(clicking phone)* Oh . . . ! *(Bland buzzing signal continues. She hangs up.)* How awful! How unspeakably . . .

   (Dialling. Phone buzz.)

First Operator   Your call, please?

Mrs Stevenson   *(unnerved and breathless, into phone)* Operator. I — I've just been cut off.

First Operator   I'm sorry, madam. What number were you calling?

Mrs Stevenson   Why — it was supposed to be Murray Hill 4-0098, but it wasn't. Some wires must have crossed — I was cut into a wrong number — and — I've just heard the most dreadful thing — a-a murder — and — *(imperiously)* Operator, you'll simply have to retrace that call at once.

First Operator I beg your pardon, madam — I don't quite —

Mrs Stevenson Oh — I know it was a wrong number, and I had no business listening — but these two men — they were cold-blooded fiends — and they were going to murder somebody — some poor innocent woman — who was all alone — in a house near a bridge. And we've got to stop them — we've got to —

First Operator *(patiently)* What number were you calling, madam?

Mrs Stevenson That doesn't matter. This was a *wrong* number. And *you* dialled it. And we've got to find out what it was — immediately!

First Operator But — madam —

Mrs Stevenson Oh — why are you so stupid? Look — it was obviously a case of some little slip of the finger. I told you to try Murray Hill 4-0098 for me — you dialled it — but your finger must have slipped — and I was connected with some other number — and I could hear them, but they couldn't hear me. Now, I simply fail to see why you couldn't make the same mistake again — on purpose — why you couldn't *try* to dial Murray Hill 4-0098 in the same careless sort of way . . .

First Operator *(quickly)* Murray Hill 4-0098? I will try to get it for you, madam.

Mrs Stevenson *(sarcastically) Thank* you. *(Sound of ringing. Busy signal.)*

First Operator I am sorry. Murray Hill 4-0098 is busy.

Mrs Stevenson *(frantically clicking receiver)* Operator, operator.

First Operator Yes, madam.

Mrs Stevenson *(angrily)* You *didn't* try to get that wrong number at all. I asked explicitly. And all you did was dial correctly.

First Operator I am sorry. What number were you calling?

Mrs Stevenson Can't you, for once, forget what number I was calling, and do something specific? Now I want to trace that call. It's my civic duty — it's *your* civic duty — to trace that call . . . and to apprehend those dangerous killers — and if *you* don't . . .

First Operator *(glancing around wearily)* I will connect you with the Chief Operator.

Mrs Stevenson PLEASE. *(Sound of ringing.)*

First Operator Miss Curtis. Will you pick up on 17, please?

Chief Operator *(middle-aged, efficient type)* Yes, dear. What's the trouble?

First Operator Somebody wanting a call traced. I can't make head nor tail of it . . .

Chief Operator Sure, dear. 17? *(Coolly and professionally.)* This is the Chief Operator.

Mrs Stevenson Chief Operator? I want you to trace a call. A telephone call. Immediately. I don't know where it came from, or who was making it, but it's absolutely necessary that it be tracked down. Because it was about a murder. Yes, a terrible, cold-blooded murder of a poor innocent woman — tonight — at eleven-fifteen.

Chief Operator I see.

Mrs Stevenson *(high-strung, demanding)* Can you trace it for me? Can you track down those men?

Chief Operator It depends, madam.

Mrs Stevenson Depends on what?

Chief Operator It depends on whether the call is still going on. If it's a live call, we can trace it on the equipment. If it's been disconnected, we can't.

Mrs Stevenson Disconnected?

Chief Operator If the parties have stopped talking to each other.

Mrs Stevenson Oh — but — but of course they must have stopped talking to each other by *now*. That was at least five minutes ago — and they didn't sound like the type who would make a long call.

Chief Operator Well, I can try tracing it. Now — what is your name, madam?

Mrs Stevenson Mrs Stevenson. Mrs Elbert Stevenson. But — listen —

Chief Operator And your telephone number?

Mrs Stevenson   *(more irritably)* Plaza 4-2295. But if you go wasting all this time —

Chief Operator   And what is your reason for wanting the call traced?

Mrs Stevenson   My reason? Well — for Heaven's sake — isn't it obvious? I overhear two men — they're killers — they're planning to murder this woman — it's a matter for the police.

Chief Operator   Have you told the police?

Mrs Stevenson   No. How could I?

Chief Operator   You're making this check into a private call purely as a private individual?

Mrs Stevenson   Yes. But meanwhile —

Chief Operator   Well, Mrs Stevenson — I seriously doubt whether we could make this check for you at this time just on your say-so as a private individual. We'd have to have something more official.

Mrs Stevenson   Oh — for Heaven's sake! You mean to tell me I can't report a murder without getting tied up in all this red tape? Why — it's perfectly idiotic. All right, then. I *will* call the police. *(She slams down the receiver.)* Ridiculous! *(Sound of dialling.)*

Second Operator   Your call, please?

Mrs Stevenson   *(very annoyed)* The Police Department — *please.*

Second Operator   Ringing the Police Department.

(Ring twice. The phone is picked up.)

Sergeant Duffy   *(picks up phone, which has rung twice)* Police Department. Precinct 43. Duffy speaking.

Mrs Stevenson   Police Department? Oh. This is Mrs Stevenson — Mrs Elbert Smythe Stevenson of 53 North Sutton Place. I'm calling to report a murder.

Sergeant Duffy   Eh?

Mrs Stevenson   I mean — the murder hasn't been committed yet. I just heard plans for it over the telephone . . . over a wrong number that the operator gave me. I've been trying to trace down the call myself, but everybody is so stupid — and I guess in the end you're the only people who could *do* anything.

Sergeant Duffy   *(not too impressed)* Yes, ma'am.

Mrs Stevenson   *(trying to impress him)* It was a perfectly *definite* murder. I heard their plans distinctly. Two men were talking, and they were going to murder some woman at eleven-fifteen tonight — she lived in a house near a bridge.

Sergeant Duffy   Yes, ma'am.

Mrs Stevenson   And there was a private patrolman on the street. He was going to go round for a beer on Second Avenue. And there was some third man — a client, who was paying to have the poor woman murdered — they were going to take her rings and bracelets — and use a knife — well, it's unnerved me dreadfully — and I'm not well . . .

Sergeant Duffy   I see. When was all this, ma'am?

Mrs Stevenson   About eight minutes ago. Oh . . . *(relieved)* then you *can* do something? You *do* understand —

Sergeant Duffy   And what is your name, ma'am?

Mrs Stevenson   *(impatiently)* Mrs Stevenson. Mrs Elbert Stevenson.

Sergeant Duffy   And your address?

Mrs Stevenson   53 North Sutton Place. *That's* near a bridge. The Queensboro Bridge, you know — and *we* have a private patrolman on *our* street — and Second Avenue —

Sergeant Duffy   And what was that number you were calling?

Mrs Stevenson   Murray Hill 4-0098. But — that wasn't the number I overheard. I mean Murray Hill 4-0098 is my husband's office. He's working late tonight, and I was trying to reach him to ask him to come home. I'm an invalid, you know — and it's the maid's night off — and I hate to be alone — even though he says I'm perfectly safe as long as I have the telephone right beside my bed.

Sergeant Duffy   *(stolidly)* Well — we'll look into it, Mrs Stevenson — and see if we can check it with the telephone company.

Mrs Stevenson   *(getting impatient)* But the telephone company said they couldn't check the call if the parties had stopped talking. I've already taken care of *that*.

Sergeant Duffy Oh — yes?

Mrs Stevenson *(high-handed)* Personally I feel you ought to do something far more immediate and drastic than just check the call. What good does checking the call do, if they've stopped talking? By the time you track it down, they'll already have committed the murder.

Sergeant Duffy Well — we'll take care of it, lady. Don't worry.

Mrs Stevenson I'd say the whole thing calls for a search — a complete

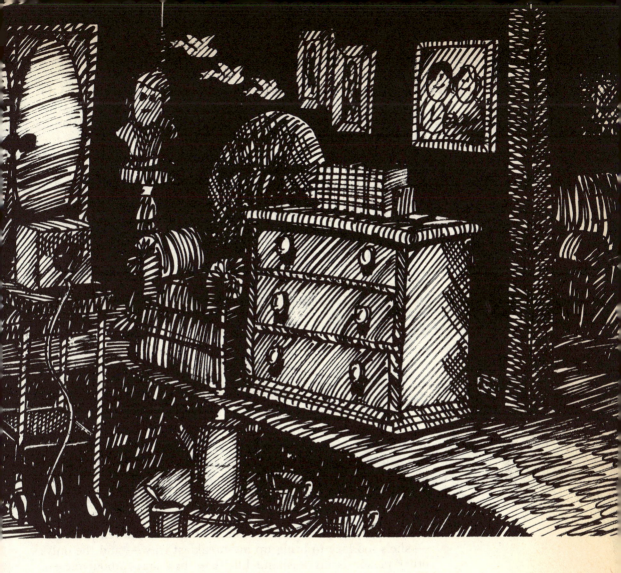

and thorough search of the whole city. I'm very near a bridge, and I'm not far from Second Avenue. And I know *I'd* feel a whole lot better if you sent around a radio car to *this* neighbourhood at once.

Sergeant Duffy And what makes you think the murder's going to be committed in your neighbourhood, ma'am?

Mrs Stevenson Oh — I don't know. The coincidence is so horrible. Second Avenue — the patrolman — the bridge . . .

Sergeant Duffy   Second Avenue is a very long street, ma'am. And do you happen to know how many bridges there are in the City of New York alone? Not to mention Brooklyn, Staten Island, Queens, and the Bronx? And how do you know there isn't some little house out on Staten Island — on some little Second Avenue you've never heard about? How do you know they were even talking about New York at all?

Mrs Stevenson   But I heard the call on the New York dialling system.

Sergeant Duffy   How do you know it wasn't a long-distance call you overheard? Telephones are funny things. Look, lady, why don't you look at it this way? Suppose you hadn't broken in on that telephone call. Suppose you'd got your husband the way you always do? Would this murder have made any difference to you then?

Mrs Stevenson   I suppose not. But it's so inhuman — so cold-blooded. . .

Sergeant Duffy   A lot of murders are committed in this city every day, ma'am. If we could do something to stop 'em, we would, But a clue of this kind that's so vague isn't much more use to us than no clue at all.

Mrs Stevenson   But, surely —

Sergeant Duffy   Unless, of course, you have some reason for thinking this call is phoney — and that someone may be planning to murder *you*?

Mrs Stevenson   *Me*? Oh — no — I hardly think so. I — I mean — why should anybody? I'm alone all day and night — I see nobody except my maid Eloise — she's a big two-hundred-pounder — she's too lazy to bring up my breakfast tray — and the only other person is my husband Elbert — he's crazy about me — adores me — waits on me hand and foot — he's scarcely left my side since I took sick twelve years ago —

Sergeant Duffy   Well — then — there's nothing for you to worry about, is there? And now — if you'll just leave the rest of this to us —

Mrs Stevenson   But what will you *do*? It's so late — it's nearly eleven o'clock.

Sergeant Duffy   *(firmly)* We'll take care of it, lady.

Mrs Stevenson   Will you broadcast it all over the city? And send out squads? And warn your radio cars to watch out — especially in suspicious neighbourhoods like mine?

Sergeant Duffy   *(more firmly)* Lady, I *said* we'd take care of it. Just now I've got a couple of other matters here on my desk that require my immediate —

Mrs Stevenson   Oh! *(She slams down receiver hard.)* Idiot.

Mrs Stevenson   *(in bed, looking at phone nervously)* Now — why did I do that? Now — he'll think I *am* a fool. Oh — why doesn't Elbert come home? *Why* doesn't he? *(Sound of dialling.)*

First Operator   Your call, please?

Mrs Stevenson   Operator — for Heaven's sake — will you ring that Murray Hill 4-0098 number again? I can't think what's keeping him so long.

First Operator   Ringing Murray Hill 4-0098. *(Ringing, busy signal.)* The line is busy. Shall I —

Mrs Stevenson   *(nastily)* I can hear it. You don't have to tell me. I know it's busy. *(Slams down receiver.)* If I could only get out of this bed for a little while. If I could get a breath of fresh air — or just lean out of the window — and see the street . . . *(The phone rings. She darts for it instantly.)* Hello. Elbert? Hello. Hello. Hello. Oh — what's the matter with this phone? HELLO? HELLO? *(Slams down receiver. The phone rings again, once. She picks it up.)* Hello? Hello . . . Oh — for Heaven's sake — who *is* this? Hello. Hello. HELLO. *(Slams down receiver, dials* **Operator**.*)*

Third Operator   Your call, please?

Mrs Stevenson   *(very annoyed and imperious)* Hello. Operator, I don't know what's the matter with this telephone tonight, but it's positively driving me crazy. I've never seen such inefficient, miserable service. Now, look. I'm an invalid, and I'm very nervous, and I'm *not* supposed to be annoyed. But if this keeps on much longer . . .

Third Operator   *(a young sweet type)* What seems to be the trouble, madam?

Mrs Stevenson   Well — everything's wrong. The whole world could be murdered, for all you people care. And now — my phone keeps ringing . . .

Third Operator Yes, madam?

Mrs Stevenson Ringing and ringing and ringing every five seconds, or so, and when I pick it up, there's no one there.

Third Operator I am sorry, madam. If you will hang up, I will test it for you.

Mrs Stevenson I don't want you to test it for me. I want you to put through that call — whatever it is — at once.

Third Operator *(gently)* I am afraid that is not possible, madam.

Mrs Stevenson *(storming)* Not possible? And why — may I ask?

Third Operator The system is automatic, madam. If someone is trying to dial your number, there is no way to check whether the call is coming through the system or not — unless the person who is trying to reach you complains to his particular operator —

Mrs Stevenson Well, of all the stupid, complicated . . . ! And meanwhile *I've* got to sit here in my bed, *suffering* every time that phone rings — imagining everything . . .

Third Operator I will try to check it for you, madam.

Mrs Stevenson Check it! Check it! That's all anybody can do. Of all the stupid, idiotic . . . ! *(She hangs up.)* Oh — what's the use . . . *(Instantly **Mrs Stevenson's** phone rings again. She picks up the receiver. Wildly)* Hello. HELLO. Stop ringing, do you hear me? Answer me! What do you want? Do you realize you're driving me crazy? Stark, staring . . .

Western Union Man *(dull flat voice)* Hello. Is this Plaza 4-2295?

Mrs Stevenson *(catching her breath)* Yes. Yes. This is Plaza 4-2295.

Western Union Man This is Western Union. I have a telegram here for Mrs Elbert Stevenson. Is there anyone there to receive the message?

Mrs Stevenson *(trying to calm herself)* I am Mrs Stevenson.

Western Union Man *(reading flatly)* The telegram is as follows:

'Mrs Elbert Stevenson. 53 North Sutton Place, New York, New York. Darling. Terribly sorry. Tried to get you for last hour, but line busy. Leaving for Boston eleven p.m. tonight on urgent business. Back tomorrow afternoon. Keep happy. Love. Signed. Elbert.'

Mrs Stevenson *(breathlessly, aghast, to herself)* Oh . . . no . . .

Western Union Man That is all, madam. Do you wish us to deliver a copy of the message?

Mrs Stevenson No — no, thank you.

Western Union Man Thank you, madam. Good night. *(He hangs up phone.)*

Mrs Stevenson *(mechanically, to phone)* Good night. *(She hangs up slowly and suddenly bursts into tears.)* No — no — it isn't true! He couldn't do it! Not when he knows I'll be all alone. It's some trick — some fiendish . . .

(She dials **Operator**.*)*

Fourth Operator *(coolly)* Your call, please?

Mrs Stevenson Operator — try that Murray Hill 4-0098 number for me just once more, please.

Fourth Operator Ringing Murray Hill 4-0098. *(The call goes through. We hear ringing at other end, ring after ring.)*

Mrs Stevenson He's gone. Oh — Elbert how could you? How could you . . .? *(She hangs up phone, sobbing pityingly to herself, turning restlessly.)* But I can't be alone tonight. I can't. If I'm alone one more second . . . I don't care what he says — or what the expense is — I'm a sick woman — I'm entitled. *(She dials* **Information**.*)*

Information This is Information.

Mrs Stevenson I want the telephone number of Henchley Hospital.

Information Henchley Hospital? Do you have the address, madam?

Mrs Stevenson No. It's somewhere in the 70's though. It's a very small, private and exclusive hospital where I had my appendix out two years ago. Henchley. H-E-N-C-

Information One moment, please.

Mrs Stevenson Please — hurry. And please — what is the time?

Information I do not know, madam. You may find out the time by dialling Meridian 7-1212.

Mrs Stevenson *(irritated)* Oh — for Heaven's sake! Couldn't you —?

Information The number of Henchley Hospital is Butterfield 7-0105, madam.

Mrs Stevenson Butterfield 7-0105. *(She hangs up before she finishes speaking, and immediately dials the number as she repeats it. The phone rings.)*

Woman *(middle-aged, solid, firm, practical)* Henchley Hospital, good evening.

Mrs Stevenson Nurses' Registry.

Woman Who was it you wished to speak to, please?

Mrs Stevenson *(high-handed)* I want the Nurses' Registry at once. I want a trained nurse. I want to hire her immediately. For the night.

Woman I see. And what is the nature of the case, madam?

Mrs Stevenson Nerves. I'm very nervous. I need soothing — and companionship. My husband is away — and I'm —

Woman Have you ever been recommended to us by any doctor in particular, madam?

Mrs Stevenson No. But I don't really see why all this catechizing is necessary. I want a trained nurse. I was a patient in your hospital two years ago. And after all, I *do* expect to *pay* this person —

Woman We quite understand that, madam. But registered nurses are very scarce just now — and our superintendent has asked us to send people out only on cases where the physician in charge feels it is absolutely necessary.

Mrs Stevenson *(growing hysterical)* Well — it *is* absolutely necessary. I'm a sick woman. I — I'm very upset. Very. I'm alone in this house — and I'm an invalid — and tonight I overheard a telephone conversation that upset me dreadfully. About a murder — a poor woman who was going to be murdered at eleven-fifteen tonight — in fact, if someone doesn't come at once — I'm afraid I'll go out of my mind . . . *(Almost off the handle by now.)*

Woman *(calmly)* I see. Well — I'll speak to Miss Phillips as soon as she comes in. And what is your name, madam?

Mrs Stevenson Miss Phillips. And when do you expect her in?

Woman I really don't know, madam. She went out to supper at eleven o'clock.

Mrs Stevenson Eleven o'clock. But it's not eleven yet. *(She cries out.)* Oh, my clock *has* stopped. I *thought* it was running down. What time is it?

Woman Just fourteen minutes past eleven . . . *(Sound of phone receiver being lifted on same line as **Mrs Stevenson's**. A click.)*

Mrs Stevenson *(crying out)* What's *that?*

Woman What was what, madam?

Mrs Stevenson That — that click just now — in my telephone? As though someone had lifted the receiver off the hook of the extension phone downstairs . . .

Woman I didn't hear it, madam. Now — about this . . .

Mrs Stevenson *(scared)* But *I* did. There's someone in this house. Someone downstairs in the kitchen . . . And they're listening to me now. They're . . . *(She hangs up the phone. In a suffocated voice.)* I won't pick it up. I won't let them hear me. I'll be quiet — and they'll think . . . *(With growing terror.)* But if I don't call someone now — while they're still down there — there'll be no time . . . *(She picks up the receiver. There is a bland buzzing signal. She dials* **Operator***. The phone rings twice.)*

Fifth Operator *(fat and lethargic)* Your call, please?

Mrs Stevenson *(a desperate whisper)* Operator — I — I'm in desperate trouble . . . I —

Fifth Operator I cannot hear you, madam. Please speak louder.

Mrs Stevenson *(still whispering)* I don't dare. I — there's someone listening. Can you hear me now?

Fifth Operator   Your call, please? What number are you calling, madam?

Mrs Stevenson   *(desperately)* You've got to hear me. Oh — please. You've got to help me. There's someone in this house. Someone who's going to murder me. And you've got to get in touch with the . . . *(Click of receiver being put down in **Mrs Stevenson's** line. She bursts out wildly.)* Oh — there it is . . . he's put down . . . he's put down the extension . . . he's coming . . . *(She screams.)* He's coming up the stairs . . . *(hoarsely)* Give me the Police Department. *(screaming)* The police! . . .

Fifth Operator   Ringing the Police Department.

   *(Phone rings. We hear the sound of a train beginning to fade in. On second ring, **Mrs Stevenson** screams again, but the roaring of train drowns out her voice. For a few seconds we hear nothing but roaring of train, then dying away, phone at police headquarters ringing.)*

Sergeant Duffy   Police Department. Precinct 43. Duffy speaking. *(Pause)* Police Department. Duffy speaking.

Second Man   Sorry. Wrong number. *(Hangs up.)*

CURTAIN

Questions

1   Mrs Stevenson is convinced that the operator made a mistake when she dialled Murray Hill 4-0098. Did she? What happened?

2   Who planned the murder in this play?

3   What was the motive for this murder?

4   Describe three personality qualities of Mrs Stevenson. Give evidence from the play to support your claims.

5   At what point did you begin to suspect that Mrs Stevenson was to be the murder victim?

6 Why does Sergeant Duffy not try to do more with the information supplied by Mrs Stevenson?

7 Why were the rings, bracelets and jewellery to be removed by the murderer?

8 Explain why the phone rings a couple of times near the end, but no-one answers when Mrs Stevenson picks it up.

9 When does Mrs Stevenson first suspect that *she* is the one to be murdered?

10 Who is it that answers the phone in the very last line of the play? Why does he say 'Sorry. Wrong number.'?

A NIGHT AT AN INN

Lord Dunsany

Cast

A. E. Scott-Fortescue (The Toff) ... A dilapidated gentleman

William Jones (Bill)
Albert Thomas } .... Merchant sailors
Jacob Smith (Sniggers)
First Priest of Klesh
Second Priest of Klesh
Third Priest of Klesh
Klesh

SCENE

The curtain rises on a room at an inn. **Sniggers** *and* **Bill** *are talking, the* **Toff** *is reading a paper.* **Albert** *sits a little apart.*

Sniggers What's his idea, I wonder?

Bill I don't know.

Sniggers And how much longer will he keep us here?

Bill We've been here three days.

Sniggers And 'aven't seen a soul.

Bill And a pretty penny it cost us when he rented the pub.

Sniggers 'Ow long did 'e rent the pub for?

Bill You never know with him.

Sniggers It's lonely enough.

Bill 'Ow long did you rent the pub for, Toffy?

(The **Toff** *continues to read a sporting paper; he takes no notice of what is said.)*

Sniggers 'E's *such* a toff.

Bill Yet 'e's clever, no mistake.

Sniggers Those clever ones are the beggars to make a muddle. Their plans are clever enough, but they don't work, and then they make a mess of things much worse than you or me.

Bill Ah!

Sniggers I don't like this place.

Bill Why not?

Sniggers I don't like the looks of it.

Bill He's keeping us here because here those niggers can't find us. The three heathen priests what was looking for us so. But we want to go and sell our ruby soon.

Albert There's no sense in it.

Bill Why not, Albert?

Albert   Because I gave those black devils the slip in Hull.

Bill   You gave 'em the slip, Albert?

Albert   The slip, all three of them. The fellows with the gold spots on their foreheads. I had the ruby then and I give them the slip in Hull.

Bill   How did you do it, Albert?

Albert   I had the ruby and they were following me . . .

Bill   Who told them you had the ruby? You didn't show it.

Albert   No. . . . But they kind of know.

Sniggers   They kind of know, Albert?

Albert   Yes, they know if you've got it. Well, they sort of mouched after me, and I tells a policeman and he says, O, they were only three poor niggers and they wouldn't hurt me. Ugh! When I thought of what they did in Malta to poor old Jim.

Bill   Yes, and to George in Bombay before we started.

Sniggers   Ugh!

Bill   Why didn't you give 'em in charge?

Albert   What about the ruby, Bill?

Bill   Ah!

Albert   Well, I did better than that. I walks up and down through Hull. I walks slow enough. And then I turns a corner and I runs. I never sees a corner but I turns it. But sometimes I let a corner pass just to fool them. I twists about like a hare. Then I sits down and waits. No priests.

Sniggers   What?

Albert   No heathen black devils with gold spots on their face. I give 'em the slip.

Bill   Well done, Albert!

Sniggers   *(after a sigh of content)* Why didn't you tell us?

Albert   'Cause 'e won't let you speak. 'E's got 'is plans and 'e thinks we're silly folk. Things must be done 'is way. And all the time I've give 'em the slip. Might 'ave 'ad one o' them crooked knives in him before now but for me who give 'em the slip in Hull.

Bill   Well done, Albert! Do you hear that, Toffy? Albert has give 'em the slip.

The Toff   Yes, I hear.

Sniggers   Well, what do you say to that?

The Toff   Oh! . . . Well done, Albert!

Albert   And what a' you going to do?

The Toff   Going to wait.

Albert   Don't seem to know what 'e's waiting for.

Sniggers   It's a nasty place.

Albert   It's getting silly, Bill. Our money's gone and we want to sell the ruby. Let's get on to a town.

Bill   But 'e won't come.

Albert   Then we'll leave him.

Sniggers We'll be all right if we keep away from Hull.

Albert We'll go to London.

Bill But 'e must 'ave 'is share.

Sniggers All right. Only let's go. *(To the **Toff**.)* We're going, do you hear? Give us the ruby.

The Toff Certainly. *(He gives them a ruby from his waistcoat pocket; it is the size of a small hen's egg. He goes on reading his paper.)*

Albert Come on, Sniggers. *(Exeunt **Albert** and **Sniggers**.)*

Bill Good-bye, old man. We'll give you your fair share, but there's nothing to do here — no girls, no halls, and we must sell the ruby.

The Toff I'm not a fool, Bill.

Bill No, no, of course not. Of course you ain't, and you've helped us a lot. Good-bye. You'll say good-bye?

The Toff Oh, yes. Good-bye. *(Still reads his paper. Exit **Bill**. The **Toff** puts a revolver on the table beside him and goes on with his papers. After a moment the three men come rushing in again, frightened.)*

Sniggers *(out of breath)* We've come back, Toffy.

The Toff So you have.

Albert Toffy . . . How did they get here?

The Toff They walked, of course.

Albert But it's eighty miles.

Sniggers Did you know they were here, Toffy?

The Toff Expected them about now.

Albert Eighty miles!

Bill Toffy, old man . . . what are we to do?

The Toff Ask Albert.

Bill If they can do things like this, there's no-one can save us but you, Toffy...I always knew you were a clever one. We won't be fools any more. We'll obey you, Toffy.

The Toff You're brave enough and strong enough. There isn't many that would steal a ruby eye out of an idol's head, and such an idol as that was to look at, and on such a night. You're brave enough, Bill. But you're all three of you fools. Jim would have none of my plans, and where's Jim? And George. What did they do to him?

Sniggers Don't, Toffy!

The Toff Well, then, your strength is no use to you. You want cleverness; or they'll have you the way they had George and Jim.

All Ugh!

The Toff Those black priests would follow you round the world in circles. Year after year, till they got the idol's eye. And if we died with it, they'd follow our grandchildren. That fool thinks he can escape from men like that by running round three streets in the town of Hull.

Albert God's truth, *you* 'aven't escaped them, because they're *'ere*.

The Toff So I supposed.

Albert You *supposed!*

The Toff   Yes, I believe there's no announcement in the Society papers. But I took this country seat especially to receive them. There's plenty of room if you dig, it is pleasantly situated, and, what is more important, it is in a very quiet neighbourhood. So I am at home to them this afternoon.

Bill   Well, *you're* a deep one.

The Toff   And remember, you've only my wits between you and death, and don't put your futile plans against those of an educated gentleman.

Albert   If you're a gentleman, why don't you go about among gentlemen instead of the likes of us?

The Toff   Because I was too clever for them as I am too clever for you.

Albert   Too clever for them?

The Toff   I never lost a game of cards in my life.

Bill   You never lost a game?

The Toff   Not when there was money in it.

Bill   Well, Well!

The Toff   Have a game of poker?

All   No thanks.

The Toff   Then do as you're told.

Bill   All right, Toffy.

Sniggers   I saw something just then. Hadn't we better draw the curtains?

The Toff   No.

Sniggers   What?

The Toff   Don't draw the curtains.

Sniggers   Oh, all right.

Bill   But, Toffy, they can see us. One doesn't let the enemy do that. I don't see why . . .

The Toff   No, of course you don't.

Bill   Oh, all right, Toffy. *(All begin to pull out revolvers.)*

The Toff *(putting his own away)* No revolvers, please.

Albert Why not?

The Toff Because I don't want any noise at my party. We might get guests that hadn't been invited. *Knives* are a different matter. *(All draw knives. The **Toff** signs to them not to draw them yet. He has already taken back his ruby.)*

Bill I think they're coming, Toffy.

The Toff Not yet.

Albert When will they come?

The Toff When I am quite ready to receive them. Not before.

Sniggers I should like to get this over.

The Toff Should you? Then we'll have them now.

Sniggers Now?

The Toff Yes. Listen to me. You shall do as you see me do. You will all pretend to go out. I'll show you how. I've got the ruby. When they see me alone they will come for their idol's eye.

Bill How can they tell like this which of us has it?

The Toff I confess I don't know, but they seem to.

Sniggers What will you do when they come in?

The Toff I shall do nothing.

Sniggers What?

The Toff They will creep up behind me. Then, my friends, Sniggers and Bill and Albert, who gave them the slip, will do what they can.

Bill All right, Toffy. Trust us.

The Toff If you're a little slow, you will see enacted the cheerful spectacle that accompanied the demise of Jim.

Sniggers Don't, Toffy. We'll be there, all right.

The Toff Very well. Now watch me.

(He goes past the windows to the inner door R. He opens it inwards, then, under cover of the open door, he slips down on his knee and closes it, remaining on the inside, appearing to have gone out. He signs to the others, who understand. Then he appears to re-enter in the same manner.)

Now, I shall sit with my back to the door. You go out one by one, so far as our friends can make out. Crouch very low to be on the safe side. They mustn't see you through the window.

*(**Bill** makes his sham exit.)*

Remember, no revolvers. The police are, I believe, proverbially inquisitive.

*(The other two follow **Bill**. All three are now crouching inside the door R. The **Toff** puts the ruby beside him on the table. He lights a cigarette. The door at the back opens so slowly that you can hardly say at what moment it began. The **Toff** picks up his paper. A native of India wriggles along the floor ever so slowly, seeking cover from chairs. He waves L., where the **Toff** is. The three sailors are R. **Sniggers** and **Albert** lean forward. **Bill's** arm keeps them back. An armchair had better conceal them from the Indian. The black priest nears the **Toff**. **Bill** watches to see if any more are coming. Then he leaps forward alone – he has taken his boots off – and knifes the **Priest**. The **Priest** tries to shout, but **Bill's** left hand is over his mouth. The **Toff** continues to read his sporting paper. He never looks around.)*

Bill   *(sotto voce)* There's only one, Toffy. What shall we do?

The Toff   *(without turning his head)* Only one?

Bill   Yes.

The Toff   Wait a moment. Let me think. *(Still apparently absorbed in his paper.)* Ah, yes. You go back, Bill. We must attract another guest. . . . Now, are you ready?

Bill   Yes.

The Toff   All right. You shall now see my demise at my Yorkshire residence. You must receive guests for me.

*(He leaps up in full view of the window, flings up both arms and falls to the floor near the dead **Priest**.)*

Now, be ready.

*(His eyes close. There is a long pause. Again the door opens, very, very slowly. Another **Priest** creeps in. He has three golden spots upon his forehead. He looks round, then he creeps up to his companion and turns him over and looks inside of his clenched hands. Then he looks at the recumbent **Toff**. Then he creeps towards him. **Bill** slips after him and knifes him like the other with his left hand over his mouth.)*

Bill   *(sotto voce)* We've only got two, Toffy.

The Toff   Still another.

Bill   What'll we do?

The Toff   *(sitting up)* Hum.

Bill   This is the best way, much.

The Toff   Out of the question. Never play the same game twice.

Bill   Why not, Toffy?

The Toff   Doesn't work if you do.

Bill   Well?

The Toff   I have it, Albert. You will now walk into the room. I showed you how to do it.

Albert   Yes.

The Toff   Just run over here and have a fight at this window with these two men.

Albert   But they're . . .

The Toff   Yes, they're dead, my perspicuous Albert. But Bill and I are going to resuscitate them . . . come on.

*(**Bill** picks up a body under the arms.)*

That's right, Bill. *(Does the same.)* Come and help us, Sniggers. . . . *(**Sniggers** comes.)* Keep low, keep low. Wave their arms about Sniggers. Don't show yourself. Now, Albert, over you go. Our Albert is slain. Back you get, Bill. Back, Sniggers. Still, Albert. Mustn't move when he comes. Not a muscle.

*(A face appears at the window and stays for some time. Then the door opens and, looking craftily round, the third **Priest** enters. He looks at his companions' bodies and turns round. He suspects something. He takes*

*up one of the knives and with a knife in each hand he puts his back to
the wall. He looks to the left and right.)*

Come on, Bill.

*(The **Priest** rushes to the door. The **Toff** knifes the last **Priest** from
behind.)*

A good day's work, my friends.

Bill   Well done, Toffy. Oh, you are a deep one!

Albert   A deep one if ever there was one.

Sniggers   There ain't any more, Bill, are there?

The Toff   No more in the world, my friend.

Bill   Aye, that's all there are. There were only three in the temple.
Three priests and their beastly idol.

Albert   What is it worth, Toffy? Is it worth a thousand pounds?

The Toff   It's worth all they've got in the shop. Worth just whatever
we like to ask for it.

Albert   Then we're millionaires now.

The Toff Yes, and, what is more important, we no longer have any heirs.

Bill We'll have to sell it now.

Albert That won't be easy. It's a pity it isn't small, and we had half a dozen. Hadn't the idol any other on him?

Bill No, he was green jade all over and only had this one eye. He had it in the middle of his forehead and was a long sight uglier than anything else in the world.

Sniggers I'm sure we ought to be very grateful to Toffy.

Bill And, indeed, we ought.

Albert If it hadn't been for him . . .

Bill Yes, if it hadn't been for old Toffy . . .

Sniggers He's a deep one.

The Toff Well, you see, I just have a knack of foreseeing things.

Sniggers I should think you did.

Bill Why, I don't suppose anything happens that our Toff doesn't foresee. Does it, Toffy?

The Toff Well, I don't think it does, Bill. I don't think it often does.

Bill Life is no more than just a game of cards to our old Toff.

The Toff Well, we've taken these fellows' tricks.

Sniggers *(going to the window)* It wouldn't do for anyone to see them.

The Toff Oh, nobody will come this way. We're all alone on a moor.

Bill Where will we put them?

The Toff Bury them in the cellar, but there's no hurry.

Bill And what then, Toffy?

The Toff Why, then we'll go to London and upset the ruby business. We have really come through this job very nicely.

Bill I think the first thing that we ought to do is to give a little supper to old Toffy. We'll bury these fellows tonight.

Albert Yes, let's.

Sniggers   The very thing!

Bill   And we'll all drink his health.

Albert   Good old Toffy!

Sniggers   He ought to have been a general or a premier.

(They get bottles from cupboard, etc.)

The Toff   Well, we've earned our bit of a supper.

(They sit down.)

Bill   *(glass in hand)* Here's to old Toffy, who guessed everything!

Albert and **Sniggers**   Good old Toffy!

Bill   Toffy, who saved our lives and made our fortunes.

Albert and **Sniggers**   Hear! Hear!

The Toff   And here's to Bill, who saved me twice tonight.

Bill   Couldn't have done it but for your cleverness, Toffy.

Sniggers   Hear, hear! Hear, hear!

Albert   He foresees everything.

Bill   A speech, Toffy. A speech from our general.

All   Yes, a speech.

Sniggers   A speech!

The Toff   Well, get me some water. This whisky's too much for my head, and I must keep it clear till our friends are safe in the cellar.

Bill   Water? Yes, of course. Get him some water, Sniggers.

Sniggers   We don't use water here. Where shall I get it?

Bill   Outside in the garden. *(Exit **Sniggers**.)*

Albert   Here's to future!

Bill   Here's to Albert Thomas, Esquire.

Albert   And William Jones, Esquire.

*(Re-enter **Sniggers**, terrified.)*

The Toff   Hullo, here's Jacob Smith, Esquire, JP, alias Sniggers, back again.

Sniggers   Toffy, I've been thinking about my share in that ruby. I don't want it, Toffy; I don't want it.

The Toff   Nonsense, Sniggers. Nonsense.

Sniggers   You shall have it, Toffy, you shall have it yourself, only say Sniggers has no share in this 'ere ruby. Say it, Toffy, say it!

Bill   Want to turn informer, Sniggers?

Sniggers   No, no. Only I don't want the ruby, Toffy . . .

The Toff   No more nonsense, Sniggers. We're all in together in this. If one hangs, we all hang; but they won't outwit me. Besides, it's not a hanging affair, they had their knives.

Sniggers   Toffy, Toffy, I always treated you fair, Toffy. I was always one to say, 'Give Toffy a chance.' Take back my share, Toffy.

The Toff   What's the matter? What are you driving at?

Sniggers   Take it back, Toffy.

The Toff   Answer me, what are you up to?

Sniggers   I don't want my share any more.

Bill   Have you seen the police? (**Albert** *pulls out his knife.*)

The Toff   No, no knives, Albert.

Albert   What, then?

The Toff   The honest truth in open court, barring the ruby. We were attacked.

Sniggers   There's no police.

The Toff   Well, then, what's the matter?

Bill   Out with it.

Sniggers   I swear to God . . .

Albert   Well?

The Toff   Don't interrupt.

Sniggers   I swear I saw something *what I didn't like.*

The Toff   What you didn't like?

Sniggers   *(in tears)* Oh, Toffy, Toffy, take it back. Take my share. Say you take it.

The Toff   What has he seen?

*(Dead silence, only broken by **Sniggers's** sobs. Then steps are heard. Enter a hideous **idol**. It is blind and gropes its way. It gropes its way to the ruby and picks it up and screws it into a socket in the forehead. **Sniggers** still weeps softly, the rest stare in horror. The **idol** steps out, not groping. Its steps move off, then stop.)*

The Toff   O, great heavens!

Albert   *(in a childish, plaintive voice)* What is it, Toffy?

Bill   Albert, it is that obscene idol *(in a whisper)* come from India.

Albert   It is gone.

Bill   It has taken its eye.

Sniggers   We are saved.

A voice off   *(with outlandish accent)* Meestaire William Jones, Able Seaman.

*(The **Toff** has never spoken, never moved. He only gazes stupidly in horror.)*

Bill   Albert, Albert, what is this? *(He rises and walks out. One moan is heard. **Sniggers** goes to the window. He falls back, sickly.)*

Albert   *(in a whisper)* What has happened?

Sniggers   I have seen it. I have seen it. Oh, I have seen it! *(He returns to table.)*

The Toff   *(laying his hand very gently on **Sniggers's** arm, speaking softly and winningly)* What was it, Sniggers?

Sniggers   I have seen it.

Albert   What?

Sniggers   Oh!

Voice   Meestaire Albert Thomas, Able Seaman.

Albert   Must I go, Toffy? Toffy, must I go?

Sniggers   *(clutching him)* Don't move.

Albert   *(going)* Toffy, Toffy. *(Exit.)*

Voice   Meestaire Jacob Smith, Able Seaman.

Sniggers   I can't go, Toffy, I can't go. I can't do it. *(He goes.)*

Voice   Meestaire Arnold Everett Scott-Fortescue, late Esquire, Able Seaman.

The Toff   I did not foresee it. *(Exit.)*

CURTAIN

Questions

1   What indications are there at the start of the play that the men are tired of waiting?

2   Why are the priests following these men?

3   What early signs are there that the Toff is a cool customer?

4   Why did the Toff select this inn to wait in?

5   Why is the Toff gently sarcastic towards Albert during the play?

6   Why does the Toff insist on no revolvers?

7   What is the first indication that all is not finished, although the priests are dead?

8   What is the Toff's real name?

9   Explain what happens at the end. Whose voice calls their names?

10   What is the mistake that the Toff has made?

The Sky is Overcast

Anthony Booth

Cast

Max Benoir
Janine..............................His wife
Maman ....His mother
Marie..............................His sister
Ronald Sedge ....Pilot Officer, RAF
Oberleutnant Muller........German Security Officer
Marcel Courant
Announcer

SCENE

A September evening, 1943, in the kitchen of **Max Benoir's** *cottage in northern France during the German occupation. As the curtain rises the room is faintly lit by the fading sunset and the dull light from the fire.* **Maman** *sits in the rocking chair. An embittered old woman of sixty-five, she knits ceaselessly and rarely speaks.* **Janine Benoir,** *a young, attractive woman, is preparing supper by the fire. She tastes some of the soup then replaces the lid on the saucepan. She crosses to the dresser, takes some small plates and spoons and starts to lay them on the table. As she does so there is the sound of a dog barking in the distance. She crosses to the window and peers out. Apparently seeing nothing of interest she returns to the dresser, collects a long loaf and places it upon the table, then after a cursory inspection goes to the door L. and calls.*

Janine Max.

Max *(offstage)* Yes.

Janine Supper is nearly ready.

Max Good.

> *(The door R. opens and* **Marie,** *a girl of about twenty-five, enters. She is expecting a child but is not too obviously pregnant. She struggles with a heavy wooden pail of water.* **Janine** *sees her and crossing quickly takes the pail from her.)*

Janine You little fool! Do you want to lose your baby?

Marie I can manage.

Janine Of course you can't. *(She takes the pail and places it beside the fire.* **Marie** *goes and sits wearily at the chair R. of the table. She buries her face in her hands for a few seconds.)*

Marie I wouldn't mind if I did lose it.

Janine Marie!

Marie What have *I* got to look forward to?

Maman *(quietly)* Everything, my child.

Marie *(turns to her)* Everything? What do you know about it, you have had your life. You haven't got to worry about bringing a child

... bringing a child into the world a prisoner with practically nothing to eat, nothing to wear and nothing but misery ahead of it.

Maman   You forget you were born in nearly the same circumstances nearly twenty-five years ago. I faced the same things as you but I did not despair. You were born and I was proud and happy to have you. For me it was worse because your father had been killed. You have got your man still.

Marie   How do I know? For five months, no word, nothing.

Maman   You would know if anything had happened. Bad news travels fast.

Marie   *(desperately)* But how can I be sure?

*(**Max Benoir** enters quietly L. He is a fine looking man of about thirty-five. He stands in the doorway for a few moments watching **Marie** while he dries his hands on the remaining shreds of a towel.)*

Max   How can you be sure of what?

Janine   Marie is worried about Albert. She has had no news for months.

Max   Naturally.

Marie   Why naturally? There must be a reason.

Max   Of course there is.

Marie   And I know what it is. He's dead . . . He's dead, isn't he? Why won't you tell me the truth?

*(She moves away from the table with her back to him and starts to sob. **Max** glances at **Janine**, throws the towel away and goes to her. He takes her shoulders almost roughly and turns her to face him.)*

Max   Listen you little fool and I'll tell you why you have not heard from Albert.

Marie   *(quietly)* Yes?

Max   He won't get in touch with you because if he did he would run the risk of exposing himself.

Marie   But if he loves me . . .

Max   If it were only himself it would be worth it but he is also thinking of the lives of a hundred men who work with him. Men who work in forests, live in dirty caves and practically starve in order to light the flare paths at night so that the RAF can drop us guns, ammunition, mines, medical supplies . . . everything to enable us to fight. *(He pauses for a moment and she half turns away ashamed of her outburst. He continues quietly.)* Some of these men have not seen their women for over a year but they still keep faith with their comrades. They make no attempt to communicate with those at home because one mistake can smash the whole organisation. *(kindly)* Now do you understand?

(There is a little silence. She looks up at him.)

Marie   I'm sorry, Max . . . I did not realise.

Max   *(smiles and ruffles her hair)* Don't worry my little one, your Albert is safe enough.

Marie   *(impulsively)* Max, you are not lying?

Max   No, I am not lying. He's well and doing good work.

Marie   *(almost whispering)* Thank you Max.

(He smiles at her then moves to the window and gazes out.)

Janine   *(brightly)* Oh, I nearly forgot. I have a surprise for you. I found some wool today and white wool too.

Marie   Oh Jan!

Janine   Of course it has been used and it is still made up in a jersey or something, but you can soon unpick it. There will be plenty to finish that little coat and make another one. I have started to undo it for you.

Marie   Oh thank you, Jan.

Janine   I have left it on my bed. You will have to wash it of course.

Marie   *(smiles)* I will get it now.

*(She starts to go out of the door L., pauses in the doorway then runs to **Janine** and hugs her passionately for a moment before running out. **Max** continues to stare out of the window; he passes his hand across his forehead wearily. **Janine** watches him curiously for a moment.)*

Janine *(quietly)* Max, was it true about Albert?

Max Was what true?

Janine Is he alive?

Max I don't know.

Janine *(surprised)* You don't know! But you said . . .

Maman He said he did not know.

Max *(turns and faces her wearily)* I had to tell her something. I told her what she wanted to hear.

Janine There is no news at all then?

Max No, nothing. I am expecting Marcel from Saumur tonight, perhaps he can give us some information.

Janine How will he get through?

Max It is all arranged. *(He moves to the top of the table and starts to break the bread into rough sections. His mood changes, he is almost gay.)* Oh by the way, where did you get that wool for Marie?

Janine *(guiltily)* From . . . from your chest of drawers.

Max From my . . .

Janine Yes, it's the old woollen vest I knitted for you to wear in the boat.

Max Is it? And what am I expected to wear now?

Janine You don't need it my darling.

Max Yes, but . . .

Janine *(she smiles at him and affectionately buttons his shirt)* It isn't much to give for a little happiness, Max.

Max *(smiles and kisses the top of her head)* Perhaps not.

Janine *(quietly)* Thank you.

Max *(teasing her)* Let's have some of your vile soup. What is it tonight, turnip?

Janine No, mangel. But it is good though. Smell. *(She brings the saucepan and takes the lid off. He smells and shudders.)*

Max Ugh! . . . Oh by the way, is there any oil left in the lamp?

Janine *(shakes it)* A little.

Max Light it, will you? Let us have a celebration Maman, we have not had turnip soup for two nights now.

> *(**Maman** gets up and crosses to the window. While **Janine** lights the lamp she closes the curtains. **Janine** lays three bowls of soup on the table leaving the fourth to keep warm beside the fire. They sit down at the table, **Max** at the head, **Maman** on his right and **Janine** on his left. **Max** murmurs a short grace and they cross themselves. For a little while they eat in silence, then there is the sound of heavy bombers overhead. **Max** glances at his watch.)*

Max They are early tonight . . . Turn that light down. *(**Janine** does so and stands in front of it to shield the light. **Max** goes to the window, carefully pulls the curtains aside then gazes upwards.)* They are turning east.

Janine How many, Max?

Max Difficult to say but it looks like a big raid. I should think about a thousand from the sound of them. *(quietly)* Vive le sport, mes amis.

> *(He closes the curtains and **Janine** turns up the light again. He stands for a moment lost in thought, straightening a loose cigarette he has found in his pocket. During the whole of this little scene **Maman** has taken no notice but continued quietly with her supper.)*

Maman Come and get your supper Max.

Max I'm not hungry Maman, you have my share.

Janine But you must eat.

Max Later perhaps.

Janine *(goes to him a little worried)* Darling, you are not ill?

Max *(gives a short laugh)* No my little one, just anxious . . . That's funny!

Janine What?

Max They are not firing on the planes.

Janine *(listens)* No, they are not.

(While she listens he wanders down below the table to the fire. Janine watches him a little puzzled.)

Janine   What are you worried about. Marcel?

Max   Yes.

Maman   He will be all right, he's no fool.

Max   Neither are the Bosche.

Janine   You said it was all arranged.

Max   So it is.

Janine   Then why are you worried?

Max   I always worry until they arrive. Eat your supper, it is getting cold.

(She sits at the table again with her back to him. He takes a paper spill from a vase on the mantelpiece, holds it to the lamp and lights his cigarette. He smothers the spill quickly and unrolls it. It is a notice of some kind.)

Max   *(smiling)* These Bosche notices come in handy. *(He reads.)* 'Penalty for harbouring the enemy or aiding escape in any form, death by shooting. Signed, Hans Scheikart, Commandant.' Funny how they always insist on making everything legal.

Maman   They were the same in the last war.

Max   When the Gestapo get a lead on us they will have to do a lot of shooting, I'm thinking.

Janine   *(putting her spoon down with a rattle against her plate)* Max, don't talk like that.

Max   Why not? It's true, isn't it?

Janine   Yes I know but . . .

Max   They shot nine of our men at Nantes last week, the swine.

Maman   Has that made any difference to us?

Max   From here to Brest, no. But I can't say from here to Nantes. That is something else that Marcel may be able to tell us. Why doesn't he come, he should have been here two hours ago.

Maman   Is it very important, his visit?

Max   Yes. I must have the new contacts between here and Nantes and above all he has the details of the next rendezvous. Until I have that information I cannot make a plan.

(There is an urgent but low knocking at the door.)

Maman   Here he is.

*(The door opens quickly and **Ronald Sedge** enters. He is a Pilot Officer in the RAF. He wears battle dress which is a little muddy, and flying boots. He has lost his hat and it is obvious that he has been running to avoid patrols. He leans against the door listening to find out if he has been followed.)*

Max   What do you want?

Sedge   *(turns his head but still listens)* Shelter for a short time. Phew! I thought that ruddy sentry would never leave the edge of the field.

Janine   *(almost hysterically)* You can't stay here.

Max   *(sharply)* Jan!

*(Ignoring them, **Sedge** crosses to the window and peers carefully through the curtains. He speaks with his back to them.)*

Sedge   Don't worry, I won't embarrass you by staying. All I want is something to eat and drink, if you can spare it. *(He turns and faces them. **Max** looks at him for a few seconds then nods to the table.)*

Max   Help yourself.

Sedge   Thanks.

*(They watch him as he goes and sits rather embarrassed in **Max's** chair. **Max** turns to his mother, who is still eating.)*

Max   Maman, the door.

*(**Maman** throws her spoon down, annoyed at having her supper disturbed. She moves to the door almost protesting. **Janine** does not look at the airman but rises abruptly. Staring straight ahead, she turns to the fire and busies herself with the pots. **Max** walks quietly round the back of the table watching his visitor until he is in front of the window. **Sedge** is rather bewildered by this quiet movement all round him. He looks first at one and then at*

*the others but gets nothing in return. **Maman** in the meantime has gone outside the door for an instant. She returns closing the door after her.)*

Maman   It is all right.

*(She places the wooden bar across the door then goes and sits in her chair down R. Having done so she continues to knit as if nothing had happened. At this moment **Marie** enters L. She does not notice the airman.)*

Marie   Oh Jan, about that wool . . . *(She stops as she sees the stranger.)*

Sedge   Hullo.

Marie   *(slowly)* Hullo.

Sedge   I just dropped in, haven't had time to introduce myself yet.

Max   We'll come to that.

Janine   *(quickly)* Marie, go to the top room and keep watch by the window. If you see anyone coming this way knock on the floor.

*(As she makes a move to go **Sedge** gets quickly to his feet and takes her wrist, holding it.)*

Sedge   On second thoughts, stay down here with us, it is cosier.

Janine   *(her voice rising)* But we must keep watch.

Sedge   Or warn the Jerries? Let's play safe, shall we, and all stay here?

*(**Marie** looks at **Max** who motions her aside. She goes and sits on a stool above the fireplace.)*

Max   Now, my friend, for a few details.

*(**Sedge** is quite at ease; he stands facing **Max** with his hands in pockets.)*

Sedge   Fire ahead.

Max   What is your name?

Sedge   Sedge. What is yours?

Max   That does not matter. What is your first name?

Sedge   Ronald.

Max   Nickname?

Sedge   Ron.

Max   Have you any papers?

Sedge   Of course.

Max   Let me have them.

>   (**Sedge** *crosses to him and gives him his identity card and discs.*)

Max   Is that all?

Sedge   That is all we are allowed to carry on operations.

Max   I see. (**Max** *examines the card and compares the photo with* **Sedge**. *He nods to the chair and says kindly:*) Sit down.

Sedge   Thanks. (*He goes back to his seat and does so.* **Max** *eyes him critically for a moment then starts his cross-examination. He shoots the questions at him with increasing speed.*)

Max   Where were you born?

Sedge   Worthing.

Max   Address?

Sedge   Pentlands, Mill Road.

Max   Describe Worthing.

Sedge   Well . . . it's a South Coast town, it has a pier, two railway stations . . . nice houses . . . a promenade . . . two or three cinemas.

Max   Give me the name of the two biggest shops.

Sedge   I can't remember, I haven't lived there for twenty years.

Max   I see. Are you married?

Sedge   Yes.

Max   What is your wife's name?

Sedge   Joan.

Max   Where is she living?

Sedge   She is in the ATS.

Max   Rank?

Sedge   Corporal.

Max   When were you married?

Sedge   Three months ago.

Max   *(moving to him)* Where?

Sedge   Caxton Hall, London.

Max   What did she wear?

Sedge   A blue dress.

Max   *(almost behind him)* Any children?

Sedge   *(looking up at him)* I've only been married three months, remember?

*(**Max** smiles for a moment, realising that his trap has not worked. He moves behind **Sedge** until he is on his L. He starts again.)*

Max   How long have you been in the air force?

Sedge   Since 1939.

Max   Where were you stationed?

Sedge   Biggin Hill.

Max   What were you flying?

Sedge   Hurricanes.

Max   What are you flying now?

Sedge   I can't tell you.

Max   I understand.

Sedge   Why all these questions?

*(**Max** picks up the half-burnt leaflet from the mantelpiece and tosses it on the table in front of **Sedge**.)*

Max   Read that.

*(While **Sedge** picks it up he crosses behind him to the window and peers cautiously through the curtains. **Sedge** starts to read the leaflet but the light is bad. He glances towards the mantelpiece and **Janine**, realising that she is standing in front of the lamp, moves a little downstage, still with her back to him. **Sedge** reads the paper and frowns.)*

Sedge   I see.

Max   *(at window)* If I help you, and I don't say that I will, I've got to know all about you, my friend. An RAF uniform does not necessarily make you British.

Sedge I suppose not, but I think . . .

Max   *(coming down C.)* I am not interested in what you think. How did you come to this country?

Sedge *(irritated)* Well it wasn't on a cheap day excursion. *(**Janine** turns round and faces him belligerently. **Sedge** realises that these are not the tactics to adopt with people who are trying to help him, he is quickly penitent.)* Sorry, I was shot down. *(**Janine** turns away again.)*

Max   Where?

Sedge Not far from here.

Max   *(persisting)* Where?

Sedge *(annoyed again)* How the hell do I know, I didn't make a programme.

Max   What happened to your plane?

Sedge It went into the drink.

Max *(puzzled)* The drink?

Sedge The sea.

Max *(starting to move towards him again)* When did this happen?

Sedge About half an hour ago.

Max What did you do with your parachute?

Sedge I buried it.

Max Where?

Sedge *(impatiently)* Oh for heaven's sake, it was in a field, that's all I know.

Max *(almost behind him)* What was growing in it?

Sedge Grass I suppose, I was too busy to take much notice. No, wait a minute . . . it was turnips or something and there was an old galvanised-iron shed in the corner with lobster pots in it.

*(There is a quick interchange of looks between **Max** and **Janine**.)*

Janine Michel's field!

*(Max turns and wanders away towards **Maman**. As he walks he asks almost casually.)*

Max   Have you any tattoo marks?

Sedge   No.

*(Max turns and faces **Sedge** then says quietly.)*

Max   Come here.

*(Sedge hesitates. He glances at **Janine** then at **Max**. It is a tense moment and he does not know what is coming next. He moves slowly to within two feet of **Max**. **Max** makes a sudden movement to search him. **Sedge**, thinking he is going to strike him, starts back slightly. **Max** smiles, shrugs his shoulders indicating that he merely wishes to search him. **Sedge** relaxes and stands there. **Max** runs his hands over **Sedge's** uniform feeling inside his legs and putting his hands into the flying boots. Apparently satisfied that the man is unarmed he straightens up.)*

Max   Take your jacket off.

Sedge   Why should I?

Maman   Do as he says, young man.

(Sedge eyes them for a moment then does so. He drops it on the back of the chair.)

Sedge   *(sarcastically)* Anything else?

Max   Yes, the pullover.

*(Sedge shrugs his shoulders and takes off the roll-neck sweater he is wearing under his tunic. As he does so **Max** goes to him quickly and opens his shirt. He stares intently at **Sedge's** shoulders.)*

Sedge   What are you looking for?

Max   The marks of your parachute straps.

Sedge   Satisfied?

Max   *(grins)* Yes.

Sedge   Can I dress now?

Max   Certainly.

Sedge   Anything else?

Max   Yes. Why did you come here especially?

Sedge   No special reason. I tried two places before this. One had a dog which threatened to rouse the whole village and the other place was locked. *(He puts on his pullover. **Max** hands him his jacket and glances at it suspiciously.)*

Max   How did you get mud on your jacket, it has not rained for over a fortnight.

Sedge   I hid in a ditch to avoid a patrol.

*(**Max** is satisfied that he is genuine. He holds out his hand.)*

Max   Welcome my friend, you'll do.

(The tension over, the whole family break into smiles. One can almost sense the relief.)

Sedge   Phew! That's a relief. And now, what is *your* name?

Max   *(smiles)* That still does not matter. Get some food in you, you may go hungry tomorrow.

Sedge   Thanks, I will. *(**Sedge** moves to his old seat and sits down. **Max** goes out L. behind him.)*

Janine   Don't have that, it must be cold by now; here, take this.

(She gives him the bowl from beside the fire.)

Sedge   Thank you, you are very kind.

Janine   *(looking at him)* Not really. Let us say, we share a common hate.

Sedge   That is true.

*(**Janine** moves up to the dresser and **Sedge** starts his soup. **Marie** obviously wishes to be sociable. She takes a piece of bread from the mantelpiece and offers it to him timidly.)*

Marie   Bread?

Sedge   Thank you.

(She stares at him while he eats. He looks up a little embarrassed.)

Sedge   What are you staring at?

Marie You.

Sedge Yes I know, but why?

Marie You look so like my husband.

(Janine comes down R. of Sedge and looks at him with new interest.)

Sedge Do I?

Marie Yes. When I first came in I thought . . .

Sedge It was him? *(kindly)* I'm sorry, it must have been a disappointment.

Marie Yes.

Sedge Where is he now?

Marie With the Maquis.

Sedge The Maquis? They are brave those fellows.

Marie *(softly)* Yes, and desperate too. *(She sits on the chair on Sedge's left.)*

Sedge *(changing the subject)* What delicious soup.

Janine You *really* like it?

Sedge It's wonderful.

Janine Oh why didn't I marry YOU.

Sedge I beg your pardon?

Janine You liked my soup and it is only mangel.

Sedge *(tactlessly)* Oh well, you enjoy anything if you are really hungry.

Janine Oh!

Sedge Oh dear, now I've put my foot in it.

Maman That probably accounts for the taste.

Janine Oh Maman!

(Sedge takes out his cigarette case and offers it to Janine.)

Sedge Will you smoke?

Janine No, but I will take one for my husband if I may.

Sedge   What about the others?

Janine   No thank you, you keep them.

Sedge   Cheap round.

Maman   What is that?

Sedge   Well, it is an expression we have in England meaning . . . well, it means it has not cost you anything.

Maman   *(smiling for the first time)* No wonder they call you the mad English.

Sedge   Yes I suppose so.

Marie   Tell me about England.

Sedge   What do you want to know?

Marie   What do the women wear?

Sedge   Well . . . the smart sort of things you wear.

Marie   Are they smart?

Sedge   Yes I suppose they are, but not as smart as the French women.

Janine   That is very *galant* of you.

Sedge   Not really, I'm just repeating what the French designers always tell us in Vogue.

Janine   *(pronouncing it like **Sedge**)* Vogue?

Sedge   A very expensive women's magazine.

Janine   *(Understanding, she pronounces it the French way.)* Ah, Vogue.

Marie   Tell me about the princesses, what are they like?

Sedge   I have never seen them but in their pictures they are always beautiful.

*(**Janine** sees that a pan is about to boil over, she crosses behind the table and takes it off the fire.)*

Marie   And the Queen, I do admire her so.

Sedge   Yes, she is lovely.

Marie   I am so interested. You see, I have a book of the Coronation upstairs in my room. Of course she was a . . . how you say in English . . . a commoner?

Sedge   Er . . . yes.

Marie   What was her name before her marriage? . . . No, don't tell me . . . it was . . . Bledisloe, wasn't it?

Sedge   That's right. Bledisloe.

(**Max** *enters a door L. He stands watching them.*)

Marie   In my book there are pictures, and the one that I like most I think . . .

(*She sees* **Max** *and moves guiltily in front of the table to the window seat, where she sits.* **Max** *has a bundle of clothes and a pair of shoes under his arm. He places them on the dresser. He comes down to L. of table.*)

Max   You had better get some rest. You have far to go tomorrow.

Sedge   Where?

Max   Further down the coast. You must not ask questions. We will pass you among us until a rendezvous can be arranged to get you away. You are to talk to no-one and never disclose who has helped you at any time or where you spent any particular night. Understand?

Sedge   Yes.

Max   We have a big organisation here but it can be destroyed by one fool opening his mouth. We take no risks whatever in that respect.

Sedge   Of course not.

(**Max** *picks up the bread knife and toys with it.*)

Max   There is one condition.

Sedge   Yes?

Max   That you travel in civilian clothes.

Sedge   Well, what is so difficult in that?

Max   Plenty.

Sedge   I don't understand.

Max I'll explain. It is obvious that we cannot help you to escape if you wear uniform. You will be too . . . too . . . *(he hunts for the word)*

Sedge Conspicuous?

Max Yes.

Sedge Go on.

Max So if we are to help you, it will be necessary for you to wear civilian clothes. If you are a civilian you must have papers of identity, food cards and so on.

Sedge Naturally.

Max If you are caught in uniform you will become a prisoner of war. But if you are caught as a civilian with forged papers . . .

(He flicks the knife over, catching it by the handle, then sticks it into the table.)

You will be shot. *(pointing the knife at **Sedge**)* It is for you to make the choice, my friend.

*(**Sedge** stares at him realising the importance of this. He gets up and wanders to the window trying to make a decision. During this tense silence **Max** keeps flicking the knife over and letting the handle strike the table each time.)*

Sedge *(quietly)* Give me some clothes.

Max *(curtly)* Good. *(He throws the knife on the table and takes the clothes from the dresser. He tosses them to **Sedge**.)*

Max These should fit you. What size shoes do you take?

Sedge Nine.

Max These should do then. They are a bit big but better that than small.

*(He places them without thinking on the table and then notices the disapproving look on **Janine's** face. He takes them off the table and places them on the chair at the head of the table.)*

When you change leave your uniform and boots under the mattress, we will burn them after you have gone. Here is your identity card, we will arrange for a photo for it later. From now on your name is Jean Barron.

Sedge   *(repeating it)* Jean Barron.

Max   You are a farm worker from Soissons and you have permission to visit your sick sister in Cherbourg. Here is your pass signed by the Commandant of your area. *(He hands him the document.)*

Sedge   What is the address of my sister?

Max   You don't know. All you know is that she has moved to Cherbourg and you hope to trace her through the police.

Sedge   I see.

Max   Money. Here are two thousand francs.

Sedge   Is that enough?

Max   As a farm worker you would not have more and *(smiles)* you will have little shopping to do, my friend.

Sedge   *(taking money)* Thank you.

Max   Your ration card.

Sedge   Up-to-date?

Max   To the day. Lastly here is some chocolate and some bread. *(He stretches out his hand and **Janine** gives him a small loaf which he hands to **Sedge**.)* And now I suggest you get some sleep, you have to travel thirty kilometres tomorrow and a lot of it by foot.

Sedge   This is damn good of you. Is there anything I can do for you?

Max   *(smiles)* Yes. When and if you get back, tell your people that guns and ammunition are naturally our first requirements, but we smoke as well. *(He punches **Sedge** playfully on the shoulder and crosses behind him, going over to **Maman**.)*

Sedge   I'll make sure they drop a tobacco factory on you.

Max   Good. Marie, take this officer to your room, you will sleep with Jan tonight.

Marie   *(rises from window seat)* But what about you, Max?

Max   I have work to do, I will not be needing a bed tonight.

Sedge   Can I help you?

Max   No. You get all the sleep you can, I will call you at three o'clock.

Sedge   Very well.

Marie   Will you follow me.

Sedge   Thank you. *(He goes to the chair and picks up the shoes.)*

Max   Lock the door, Marie.

   (Sedge looks up, supicious.)

Sedge   Why?

Max   Because we are always liable to be searched at a moment's notice. If this should happen you will be able to climb into the loft by the time we produce the key. You will find a trapdoor at the other end. Open it and jump into the barn, it is only about four metres.

Sedge   What is that in feet?

Max   Four metres? Oh . . . about twelve.

Sedge   That is just about enough to break my neck.

Max   What is twelve feet to a man used to jumping in thousands?

Sedge   I haven't got my parachute now.

Max   *(smiles)* Don't worry, the hay will break your fall. *(serious again)* If this should be necessary you are on your own, you realise that? We won't be able to help you.

Sedge   Of course. Good hunting.

Max   Good night.

   *(Sedge follows **Marie** out L. **Max** glances at his watch. **Janine** is a little worried.)*

Janine   You never told me you were going out tonight, Max.

Max   I may not have to, it depends upon instructions from London. It is nearly time. Jan, keep a watch on the window.

Janine   All right.

   *(She crosses to the window and sits. **Max** goes to the fireplace and takes **Maman's** work-box over to the table. He removes the sewing, etc, from*

the top, then after taking out a false bottom he very carefully lifts out a small radio. He strews an indoor aerial across the floor, then turns the radio on. There is a little static.

Maman   What message are you expecting?

Max   The sky is overcast.

Maman   The sky is overcast . . . what a perfect description of France as she is today.

Max   (*glancing at her*) Yes, I suppose it is.

(*The voice of the **announcer** comes through gradually gaining in volume.* **Max** *turns it down a little.*)

Announcer   '. . . and observers report that the marshalling yards have been out of action for the last five days following the explosion. Early yesterday morning the engine depot at Rouen was the target of saboteurs. The heavy machine shops were totally gutted and eleven locomotives completely destroyed.'

Max   (*smiling*) That was Jouet and his gang. They have been planning that for months.

(*He turns the radio down so that the voice is faint and he is able to talk through it.*)

Maman   How was it done?

Max   The actual operation was simple. They placed small but powerful explosives in the cylinder heads of the engines after they had been banked down for the night. A short fuse and voila.

(*He snaps his fingers.*)

Maman   It sound so easy.

Max   Easy! Do you think it was easy to get into a place surrounded by barbed-wire fences three metres high, all of them electrified and guarded by forty sentries?

Janine   It sounds impossible. How was it done?

Max   The RAF staged a counter-attraction by bombing the yards about two kilometres away.

Maman   Did we lose many?

Max Four dead, six wounded. *(He turns the radio up a little.)*

Announcer 'From all these operations three aircraft failed to return. *(pause)* That is the end of the news. *(pause)* And now, here are some messages for our friends in France.
The dawn awakes . . . The dawn awakes.
The gate is open . . . The gate is open.
The cloth is cut . . . The cloth is cut.
The colour is red . . . The colour is red.
The sky is overcast . . . The sky is overcast.'

*(**Max** switches off the radio.)*

Max At last.

Maman What, Max?

Max We have our orders, tomorrow night if the weather holds.

*(**Janine**, who has been peeping through the curtains, appears agitated.)*

Janine Max, there is someone coming.

Max Who is it? Can you see? *(He is quickly hiding the radio.)*

Janine Not yet. I think it is Muller . . . he is approaching the gate now . . . oh hurry Max.

Max Perhaps it is Marcel.

Janine The sentry is challenging him.

(There is a cry of 'Halt' offstage followed by a murmur of voices.)

Janine It's Muller! Hurry Max.

Max Keep your head Jan. Oh and Maman, if you don't want to get us all shot, keep your mouth shut.

Janine He's here!

Max All right, let the swine in.

*(He has replaced all the sewing things by this time and crosses quickly to the fire leaving the apparently innocent work-box on the table. **Janine** removes the wooden bar from the door and sits by the window again. The door is kicked open and **Oberleutnant Muller** enters. He is a very smooth customer, takes his time over everything and misses nothing. He kicks the door shut with the back of his foot and stands there smoking.)*

Max What is the trouble this time? Are we showing a light or something?

(Muller drops his cigarette on the floor watching it fall. He rubs it out thoughtfully with his boot.)

Muller *(smiling)* Only when your wife opened the curtains. Expecting someone?

Max No.

Muller Then why look?

Max The war has made us suspicious.

(Muller gives him a quick look but Max's face is quite expressionless. Muller crosses slowly to the table. He places his foot on the chair R. of the table then glances at the supper things.)

Muller Four bowls of soup.

Max Yes.

Muller There are only three of you. Three into four goes once and one over . . . Who is the one over?

Max My sister Marie.

Muller Where is she?

Max Upstairs sorting some clothes.

Muller Why, is she leaving?

Janine No, she is going to . . .

Muller Shut up! *(He says this viciously without turning his head. Janine stares at him frightened. He goes on again easily to Max.)* Why is she sorting clothes?

Max She is going to have a baby and is trying to make some garments for it from some of our old things.

Muller I see. Has anyone been here tonight?

Max No.

Muller *(quickly)* Don't lie.

Max I am not. Search the house if you don't believe me.

Muller   I don't need your permission.

Max   I didn't give it. If you search you do so by force, I cannot stop you.

Muller   *(smiles)* That is true. *(He takes an apple from the table, bites it, makes a wry face, throws the apple away and spits out the piece.)* Why can't you French grow decent apples?

Max   *(half smiling)* We can but those are cider apples.

Muller   Do you like them?

Max   No.

Muller   Then why do you eat them?

Max   Because we are hungry.

Muller   A farmer hungry? That is good.

Max   Did you come to discuss food?

Muller   No. *(He picks up a piece of material from the sewing basket and holds it up gazing at it.)* I had other reasons. *(They all stare while he picks up another piece.)*

Maman   Max, pass me my sewing box.

*(**Max** makes a move to do so but **Muller** leans across and takes hold of it before **Max** can quite reach it. He looks up at **Max** and smiles.)*

Muller   No. Allow me. *(He picks it up and carries it across to **Maman**, weighing it apprehensively in his hands. **Max** turns to the fireplace and snatches up the poker which he hides behind his back.)* It is very heavy for a sewing box.

Maman   Naturally. It is made from an old battery case. It is the only thing I have ever found deep enough to hold all my rubbish.

*(She takes it from him and places it on the floor at her R. side. **Muller** does not appear to be completely satisfied. He is about to pursue it further when his attention is diverted by the entrance of **Marie** L. She is very excited.)*

Marie   Max! . . . Oh . . . I . . . *(She stops as she sees **Muller**.)*

Muller   Come in. So you are Marie?

Marie   Yes.

Muller *(curtly)* Come here. *(She goes and stands opposite him, frightened.)* I have not seen you before. How long have you been in the district?

Marie Two weeks.

Muller Where were you before?

Marie At St Malo.

Muller Why did you leave?

Marie We were bombed out by the English.

Muller Do you consider yourself a military target?

Marie No.

Muller Why do you suppose they bombed innocent citizens like you?

Marie *(slowly)* We all make mistakes. *(He starts to speed up the questioning.)*

Muller Are you married?

Marie Yes.

Muller Where is your husband?

Marie   I don't know.

Muller   What do you mean, you don't know?

Marie   We had a terrible quarrel. He left me.

Muller   When was that?

Marie   A year ago.

Muller   When are you expecting your baby? (**Marie** *is taken aback by his knowledge.*)

Marie   In . . . in four months.

Muller   In four months eh? *(slowly)* And your husband left you a year ago! *(There is a silence while* **Marie** *stares at him frightened by the way she has been trapped.* **Muller** *smiles at her.)* Who is the father, a German soldier?

(A look of hatred comes into **Marie's** *face for a second and she spits into* **Muller's** *face. He is taken aback for a moment then slaps her brutally across the cheek knocking her down to the floor at* **Janine's** *feet. She sobs pitifully and* **Janine** *kneels to help her.)*

Maman   *(bitterly)* The *master race!*

> *(**Muller** whips round and raises his arm as if to strike her. She goes on knitting without flinching or even looking at him. He lowers his arm slowly.)*

Muller   Yes you old hag, the master race. And never forget it if you want to live.

> *(**Janine** takes **Marie** out L.)*

Max   Was there anything else you wanted to see me about?

Muller   *(crossing to table)* Yes. We have reason to believe that a British aviator was shot down here tonight. We think he is hiding in the neighbourhood.

Max   Have you searched other houses?

Muller   Yes.

Max   Why not search mine?

Muller   Because you French have no imagination. If you were hiding someone you would not throw open the door so wide, especially knowing the penalty for harbouring the enemy.

Max   That makes sense.

> *(There is a pause. **Muller** takes a small automatic from his pocket.)*

Muller   Ever seen one of these before?

Max   May I look?

> *(**Muller** takes out the magazine, opens the breech and clicks the trigger to make sure it is harmless. He holds it out. **Max** goes to take it but **Muller** insolently drops it on the table. There is a quick look from **Max** but **Muller** just smiles. **Max** picks up the automatic from the table and examines it.)*

Max   No, I have never seen anything like it. What is it, German?

Muller   No, British. We found a hundred last night, cleverly hidden in a haystack. *(He gives **Max** a quizzical look.)* You would not know anything about that, would you?

Max   No.

Muller   They are nice aren't they? Nothing compared with a Luger of course, but neat all the same. It is ingenious too, it is a nine millimetre which means that German ammunition fits it.

*(**Max** unconsciously has been pointing the automatic at **Muller**. **Muller** suddenly notices this and smiles.)*

What does it feel like to be pointing a gun at a German officer?

Max   Good.

Muller   *(laughs)* I like you, you have got guts.

*(He holds out his hand for the automatic but **Max** ignores it and flings it back on the table and turns his back on him. **Muller** is annoyed, he picks it up and prepares to replace the magazine. As he does so there is a gentle knock at the door. **Max** turns round but **Muller** does not look up. **Max** glances at **Janine** who is obviously frightened. There is another knock. **Muller** is still intent on replacing the magazine. He clicks it home and, still without looking up, speaks.)*

Muller   You have a visitor. Ask him to come in.

Max   Come.

*(**Muller** turns and faces the door, gun in hand. There is a pause then the door opens and **Marcel Courant** enters. He is a short, tubby little man of about forty-five. He is typically French and has a small toothbrush moustache. All his movements and gestures are quiet and it is obvious that nothing ruffles him. He wears a shabby raincoat and a beret. **Muller** sees that the visitor is apparently an inoffensive little man and puts his gun away and sits on the table.)*

Muller   Come in and close the door.

Marcel   *(unperturbed)* Hello Max, I did not know you had company.

Muller   I bet you didn't. Come here. *(**Marcel** places a small haversack on the seat below the window and takes two or three steps towards him.)* What is your name?

Marcel   Marcel Courant.

Muller   *(snaps his fingers)* Your papers.

*(**Marcel** shrugs his shoulders, he is obviously used to this daily procedure. He takes his time finding them, then hands then to **Muller**.)*

Muller   *(examining papers)* What is your job?

Marcel   I work in a welding factory at Saumur.

Muller   Show me your hands. (*Marcel holds them out but he is standing a little too far from* **Muller** *to examine them.* **Muller** *is irritated. He beckons him sharply.*) Come here, closer. (*He feels the palms of* **Marcel's** *hands critically.*) They are very soft for a man who works in a welding factory.

Marcel   I don't handle the machinery, I recruit French labour for your bosses. It is all in my papers.

Muller   What is your reason for visiting this area?

Marcel   To try and get replacements.

Muller   What replacements?

Marcel   Ten technicians to fill the jobs of the men your people shot last week. (*bitterly*) Shot without a trial.

Muller   (*giving him a quick look*) Why are you so late in arriving? It is long after curfew.

Marcel   Because the trains don't run as they used to. Someone left a bomb on the line.

Muller   Have you a letter of authority?

Marcel   Yes. (*He produces the document.*) I have to report to your Commandant tomorrow.

Muller   (*examining it*) How did you get past the sentry?

Marcel   (*simply*) I gave him some eggs. (*In spite of himself* **Muller** *smiles.* **Marcel** *continues parrot-fashion.*) I am a bachelor, I was born at Liège in 1900. I have no identifying scars or marks,. my eyes are grey, my hair is brown . . .

(*During this speech there is the sound of an air-raid siren.* **Muller** *looks up quickly. He throws* **Marcel's** *papers at him and they fall all around him.* **Marcel** *kneels to pick them up and* **Muller** *moves quickly to the telephone. He is annoyed to find an old coat hanging on it. He takes it off and throws it angrily on the floor.*)

Muller   This is German property, not a coat hanger. (*He turns the handle at the side quickly to ring through to the HQ office, then takes off the receiver.*) Hallo . . . Hallo . . . Hier Oberleutnant Muller. (*He *listens for a moment to the voice on the other end.)* Ja . . . Ja . . . Ja, you can fire now, I am coming at once. *(He replaces the receiver and turns to* **Max**.*)* Your brave friends the RAF are just coming to bomb a few more defenceless citizens. *(He crosses to the door R. and opens it. Pausing for a moment he looks back at* **Marcel**, *who is still kneeling.)* Be sure to report to the Commandant tomorrow, little man, or your hair will not be brown . . . it will be white. *(He goes out leaving the door open.)*

*(***Marcel*** closes the door and removes his coat, which he places on the window seat. He still keeps his beret on.)*

Marcel   Who is he?

Max   Muller, area security officer.

Marcel   Dangerous?

Max   He's no fool.

Marcel   How long have you been on the telephone?

Max   Since yesterday. It is a direct line to their headquarters.

Marcel   Why have they honoured your house?

Max   They have an anti-aircraft battery in the orchard at the bottom of the field.

Marcel   I see. I wondered why there was a sentry. *(to* **Maman**) Good evening Madame.

Maman   Good evening Marcel.

Marcel   Here are the knitting needles you wanted. *(He takes them from his rucksack and gives them to her.)*

Maman   You remembered. Thank you, they will be very useful.

*(***Marcel*** goes to the window and peeps through the curtains.)*

Marcel   He is out of sight. Max, I have great news.

Max   Ssh! *(He goes to the telephone and replaces the coat. From the distance there comes the sound of the anti-aircraft batteries in action.)* It may be a microphone as well. And now my friend we can talk.

*(***Janine*** enters at door L.)*

Janine   Marcel!

Marcel   Hullo Janine.

Janine   Oh I am so glad to see you. We were worried. Why are you so late?

Marcel   Some of your friends decided to blow up thirty metres of the railway track. *(smiles)* You might have asked them to wait until my train was past. *(He moves to the table and sits on the chair R. **Janine** sits opposite and **Max** stands at the head with one foot on a chair leaning forward on his elbows.)*

Max   *(almost excited)* What was it like?

Marcel   They made a good job all right. The engine was derailed as well.

Max   Fine.

Marcel   You know, engines are funny things. On a track and pulling a train they are as solid as can be, but when they leave their beloved track they fall to pieces, lots of pieces. *(They all laugh.)* Oh, I almost forgot. *(He goes to his rucksack at the window and produces a bar of chocolate.)* For you Janine. *(He throws it gently to her. She catches it and smells it like a child.)*

Janine   Chocolate! Oh, bless you, Marcel.

Marcel   And for Marie, this! *(He produces a child's rattle.)* Where is she by the way?

Janine   *(quickly serious)* She's upstairs, she will be down in a minute.

Max   How is she?

Janine   All right now, it was shock more than anything else.

Marcel   What happened?

Max   Our guest who has just left, knocked her on to the floor.

Marcel   The swine!

Max   I could have killed him.

Maman   *(bitterly)* Instead, you stood there and watched.

Max   *(flaring up)* What else could I do? I least of all can afford to be sent to a concentration camp.

*(**Marcel** senses the situation.)*

Marcel   *(soothingly)* Of course not. You did the right thing. Without you, our complete organisation this end would be lost. *(Pause.)* And now to business.

(During this speech he has been replacing the heavy wooden bar across the door. He now crosses to the table, reverses the chair and sits astride it.)

Janine   Coffee, Marcel?

Marcel   Later please. Now Max, what news from London?

*(**Janine** moves to the stool downstage of the fire and sits with her back half to the audience. She starts to grate some carrots. **Max** moves down to chair L. of table opposite **Marcel**.)*

Max   We received the message tonight. Tomorrow we may expect another consignment, but I don't know what it is.

Marcel   I'll tell you. It is a new toy they call a Sten gun. It's light, efficient and easily hidden. You can expect a hundred, also ten canisters of ammunition. Where are you going to have them dropped?

Max   *(producing map from his pocket)* Here. See this copse on the left? Above that is a valley covered with light shrubs, good for cover. If the wind is still in the south-west it should be ideal. A man here *(he points)*, here, here and here to mark the area with white torches and one man here with a red torch to advise the aircraft the line of approach. *(There is a pause while **Marcel** examines the map.)*

Marcel   Yes. Where are the nearest patrols?

Max   Here, the other side of this hill. That is all.

Marcel   What about the north side?

Max   It falls sheer away to the sea.

Marcel   It seems all right. What time is the patrol?

Max   One thirty. I am advising London that we expect the plane at one fifty.

Marcel   Supposing they slip in an extra patrol? They might after this train business tonight.

(*Janine* moves to the dresser to get a plate.)

Max   (*smiles*) Well, if they do we shall have to play your game and give them some eggs.

Janine   (*coming down a little*) Eggs?

Max   Marcel gave some to the sentry.

Janine   (*horrified*) Marcel, you didn't!

Marcel   Oh don't worry, they were bad. (*They all laugh.*) Anything else Max?

Max   No, I don't think so . . . oh yes, the new contacts between here and Nantes.

(*Marcel* crosses to the fire below the table and half kneels in front of it warming his hands. *Max* sits on the edge of the table. *Janine* is still fussing at the dresser.)

Marcel   All arranged. I will give you full details later.

Max   Good. I am going to see Mourin tonight and get him to send the signal. Oh yes, that reminds me . . . some batteries. Can you get us some replacements? His transmitter is getting very weak.

Marcel   (*thinks for a moment*) Yes . . . Verlan is coming down early next week, I will get him to bring you two.

Max   Good. And now, what news from your end?

(*Marcel* stands and faces *Max* with his back to the fire.)

Marcel   Quite successful. Our factory output has dropped forty per cent and about fifty per cent of the work is very faulty. Last month we turned out two thousand tank tracks but unfortunately they were all ten centimetres too short.

(*Janine* comes down in between them. She appears puzzled.)

Janine   (*not understanding*) Ten centimetres? That isn't very much.

Marcel   (*smiles*) No, but you see, they don't stretch. (*They all laugh quietly and* **Max** *playfully pulls* **Janine** *towards him and puts his arms round her. She rests against him as he sits there.*) This month we are having them all back again to lengthen.

Janine   So they get them the right length in the end?

Marcel   Yes, but after a delay of over two months. A delay of one day is important with the second front not far away. Two thousand tracks represent one thousand tanks; it would be worth it if it were only thirty.

Maman   What price did we pay for that?

Marcel   Ten shot and twenty-five hostages.

Maman   Poor devils.

(Janine is upset by the news and gently breaks away from Max. Marcel crosses below the table as if he is going to the window. He speaks as he moves.)

Marcel   They may not be hostages for long, we are planning a small liberation party next Tuesday. *(He stops and turns to Max.)* If necessary could you accommodate an extra six men in your area, Max?

Max   If they are spread out, yes.

Marcel   Good. Expect them any time after Wednesday. You will be able to move them down the line all right, I know for a fact that two replacements are needed at Avranches.

Max   That is correct.

(Janine is standing beside the stool above the fireplace. Marcel moves to the window and peers out cautiously. He rests one foot on the window seat, takes out cigarette papers and a pouch and proceeds to roll a cigarette during the next speech.)

Marcel   Which brings me to something very important. Some time during the coming week, you may expect a visitor. He will be dropped not far from here and will ask your assistance. His papers will be correct and with true Bosche thoroughness he will be actually dropped by a plane with British markings. To ensure his safe arrival, all the anti-aircraft batteries in this area, in fact all areas between here and Nantes, have been ordered not to fire under any provocation until the Gestapo know that he has landed safely. They have suspected for a long time that there is an escape route through here and they are doing the thing properly. They are sending one of their most experienced agents, he speaks English fluently and will probably fool you on that score; he used to be the London representative for a Berlin firm before the war. *(He licks the cigarette paper before sticking it down.)*

However, with the knowledge we have beforehand, his fluency and RAF uniform won't do him very much good.

(During this **Janine** *has been reacting to his speech. She gives one or two glances towards the bedroom and she and* **Max** *exchange several quick looks.)*

Janine   Max!

Max   *(quickly)* Did you say they planned this for next week?

Marcel   Yes, why?

Max   You are a week out, my friend. I think your visitor is here now.

Marcel   *(incredulous)* Here!

Max   An RAF officer came here tonight and asked for shelter. He is upstairs.

Marcel   So. They changed their plans and tried it a week earlier.

Max   They may not, this man may be genuine.

Janine   *(urgently)* The battery did not fire tonight, remember.

*(**Max** walks upstage towards the dresser obviously worried.)*

Max   That's true, not even when the big raid came over. *(He spots the telephone.)* What was it Muller said on the phone?

Maman   He said, 'You can fire now, I am coming at once.'

Janine   But if this man is a member of the Gestapo why did Muller come here tonight searching for him?

Marcel   Probably to make you think that the flier was genuine and trying to escape. It was a very clever move. A man asks for shelter and five minutes later the enemy enter looking for him. It is only natural that you should take him for being the genuine article.

Max   Yes . . . That is why Muller did not insist on searching the house. The last thing he wanted to do was to find the man. If he had, the whole plan would have been wasted.

Janine   But why did he choose this house?

Marcel   I don't know. *(He crosses in front of* **Max** *until he is between them.)* They probably suspect Max of being in charge of the escape route.

Janine   Oh God!

*(**Max** moves across to the window seat and picks up **Janine's** shawl.)*

Max   Jan, slip across the lane and ask Jacques if a plane was shot down into the sea near Michel's field this evening. His patrol should be back by now.

Janine   Right.

(She crosses below the table to him. He places the shawl round her shoulders and she goes to the door and takes the wooden bar off. She places her hand on the handle and glances at him appealingly for a second. He gives her an encouraging little smile and nods his head. She opens the door quickly and goes out. He shuts the door after her then goes and peeps through the curtains to make sure that she is all right. There is quite a long pause.)

Marcel   Is she all right?

Max   Yes. *(He turns away.)* I think I will make sure he is still there.

*(He makes a move towards **Marcel** who is in front of the door L.)*

Marcel   He will be there all right.

Max   How can you be sure?

Marcel   If he is genuine he won't dare leave.

Max   And if he is from the Gestapo?

Marcel   *(lights his cigarette)* It is in his interests to remain.

Max   Why?

*(**Marcel** walks down to the fire and throws his match in it.)*

Marcel   To be passed down the line through the escape route. If he has you arrested now he loses all hope of finding the remaining stops and contacts between here and Brest. *(He turns and faces him.)* No Max, it will be at the END of the line when he acts, not at the beginning.

Max   *(comes down C. a little)* Yes, you are right.

Marcel   *(sits on stool above fireplace)* Can you describe him?

Max   About average height . . . slim build, brown hair . . . small hands.

Marcel   Colour of eyes?

Max   I didn't notice.

Marcel   Did he have a small mole on his left cheek?

Max   No. Why?

Marcel   I thought it might be Hoffman, he was originally detailed for this job. Apparently it is someone else.

Max   *(curious)* How do you know all this?

Marcel   The main telephone cable from the Gestapo headquarters runs partly through a small sewer underneath the building . . . we tap every message that comes through.

Max   *(smiles)* You think of everything.

Marcel   We have to. The day the Allies land we shall fill the sewer with dynamite and a time fuse, but until then it is more useful to leave the building intact.

Maman   You will get your reward in heaven, Marcel.

Marcel   *(dryly)* Thank you, but I would rather have it in France.

Max   *(crossing to the window)* Jan should be back by now.

Marcel   Perhaps she is waiting for the sentry to pass.

*(**Marie** bursts in at the door L. She is very excited.)*

Marie   Max! . . . Max, quickly.

Max   *(coming to her)* What is it?

Marie   The flier.

Max   *(quickly)* What about him, has he gone?

Marie   No but . . .

Max   *(takes her arm roughly)* Out with it girl!

Marcel   *(beside **Marie** on her L.)* Steady Max! *(gently)* What about him, Marie?

Marie   When he first arrived I thought he was Albert, the resemblance was so striking.

Marcel   Yes.

Marie There was something else about him too . . . perhaps it was the back of his head . . . but it was something that made me feel I had seen him before somewhere.

Marcel Go on.

Marie When I took him upstairs he asked me for a towel as he wanted to wash. I took him one a few minutes later and found him stripped to the waist at the basin. On his right shoulder he has a very bad scar and when I saw that I knew where I had seen him before.

Max Where?

Marie Last summer at Dinard. I went down to the beach one afternoon to get some sea water to boil down to make salt . . .

Max *(impatiently)* Yes, yes.

Marie While I was getting it a man was nearly downed. They pulled him out of the water and laid him face down on the sand. I was quite close and I could see his back clearly.

Marcel Yes?

Marie He had the same scar!

Max What of it?

Marie *(slowly)* That man was a German office on leave!

Max Did you see his face?

Marie No.

Max Then how can you be sure?

Marie I tell you Max, I would know that scar anywhere, it is like this. *(She moves her fingers simulating almost a streak of lightning.)* Then I remembered a bad mistake he made tonight, when I was talking about the Royal family.

Marcel Yes?

Marie He said the Queen's former name was Bledisloe.

Marcel So?

Marie I should think every Englishman knows that it was Bowes-Lyon.

*(There is a pause. **Marcel** looks at **Max** who does not appear to be completely convinced. The door R. opens and **Janine** comes in quickly. She is perturbed.)*

Max   *(anxiously)* Well? *(He goes to her.)*

Janine Jacques says that a plane with British markings flew in from the south about an hour ago. It dropped someone by parachute then dipped low over the cliffs. He thought it was going to crash but the pilot flew at sea level for about a mile then returned inland in the direction of Nantes.

*(There is a long pause. **Max** still stares at **Janine** but speaks to **Marie** who is behind him.)*

Max   Did you lock the door again, Marie?

Marie   Yes.

Max   Where is the key?

Marie   Here. *(He turns to her.)*

Max   Give it to me.

*(**Marie** slowly holds out the key but **Janine** rushes past **Max** and snatches it from her, holding it behind her back. She faces **Max** frightened.)*

Janine *(almost in a whisper)* Max, what are you going to do?

Max   Give me that key.

Janine No, Max.

*(He goes to her and twists her arm so that she is forced to release it and thrusts her away sobbing so that she stumbles against the window. **Marie**, thoroughly frightened, slips out of the door L. **Max** looks at **Marcel** for a moment and oblivious of **Janine's** sobs goes to the table. He lifts up the bread knife and then as if he has suddenly made a decision walks out of the door L. **Janine** rushes to stop him but **Marcel** bars her way.)*

Janine Max . . . Max!

Marcel Steady, Janine!

(She turns on him fiercely, she is almost hysterical. Her voice comes in hard dry sobs.)

Janine Steady! . . . What do you know about it . . . don't you realise he has gone up there to kill . . . to kill in cold blood . . . in our house . . . and you say 'steady Janine'. *(She wanders to the C. a pathetic figure.)* You don't know what it is like lying in bed every night your man is out . . . wondering if he will ever get back . . . You can't know . . . only a woman can really know a thing like that . . . You don't know what it is to start with terror every time there is a knock at the door . . . every time you hear a rifle shot . . . *(She buries her face in her hands.)* I can't stand it any longer . . . I can't stand it . . . *(She falls to her knees sobbing.)* Oh God end it all . . . please end it all.

*(**Marcel** goes to her gently and kneels on one knee behind her. He takes her shoulders.)*

Marcel   Janine, my poor Janine.

Janine   You have got to stop him, Marcel.

Marcel   Janine, listen to me. I know how you feel but you have got to put all that behind you. You must understand . . . if that man leaves here tonight, Max will be shot. You and your family will be sent to a concentration camp. But that is not all. There are a hundred men between here and Brest who will die, perhaps their families too.

Janine   Marcel, don't.

Marcel   Listen. For years now we have been building up our organisations so that on the day of Liberation we shall be able to strike in force from the inside. Nothing must stand in our way. We are all fighting a common cause so that France may be free again. *(He gets up quietly and moves away towards the window.)* So that your children can be brought up in happiness, to the sound of laughter *(bitterly)* instead of the ceaseless cry of 'Sieg Heil' and tramping of boots on cobbles. *(He turns to her kindly.)* Is the price of one enemy agent too much to ask for a thing like that?

*(There is a pause. **Janine** gets to her feet slowly and walks to the table, which she leans on. She speaks almost in a whisper.)*

Janine   You talk of death as if it were nothing.

Marcel   It *is* nothing if it justifies the means.

Janine   It's all so callous . . . doesn't a human life mean anything to you any more?

Marcel No . . . we are numbers now, not personalities. For every Frenchman killed there is another to take his place. We haven't time to consider feelings . . . time is too short and there is so much to do.

(She is suddenly slightly hysterical again and she goes to him quickly.)

Janine But Marcel, they will shoot Max for this.

Marcel *(taking her arms)* They can't. By their own orders they cannot touch him.

Janine How?

Marcel You have seen the regulations haven't you? They are posted up everywhere. 'It is the duty of every Frenchman to apprehend the enemy and prevent his escape. If necessary by death.' Don't you see *(gently)* they are caught in their own trap. Max is doing his duty by the Third Reich and there is nothing they can do about it.

Janine Oh Marcel.

*(She starts to weep again and sits sobbing on the window seat. **Marcel** looks at her with pity.)*

Marcel You poor kid . . . I'm sorry . . . but war is such a dirty business.

*(At this moment **Max** appears at the door L. He has obviously had a great struggle as his shirt is torn, he has a long scratch down the side of his face and there is blood on his hand. He does not appear to notice the others but slowly takes the coat covering the telephone and drops it on the floor. The noise makes **Janine** look towards him.)*

Janine *(in a whisper)* Max!

(He turns the handle at the side of the phone, lifts the receiver and, after a pause, speaks. His voice is quiet but it is obvious that he is going through a great emotional strain.)

Max Hullo . . . Hullo . . . Herr Commandant? This is Max Benoir . . . I found a British officer hiding in my house. He must have climbed in by the loft . . . *(He looks at **Marcel**.)* He tried to escape . . . so I killed him. Will you send some men to collect the body?

*(He replaces the receiver slowly. **Janine** sobs quietly as the CURTAIN falls slowly.)*

Questions

1 Describe the setting of the play. (Mention time and place.)

2 What sort of work does Max do in the Maquis (French Resistance)?

3 Why is Marie anxious and upset at the beginning of the play?

4 How does Max calm her down?

5 How do we know that food and supplies are short?

6 Why does Max question Sedge so closely?

7 In what other ways does Max try to check on Sedge?

8 Where is the illegal radio hidden, and why is it so important to the Maquis?

9 What are the *apparent* and what are the *real* reasons for Muller's visit to the farmhouse?

10 Why does Marcel call on Max? How does he allay Muller's suspicions?

11 Describe the gradual steps by which we discover Sedge is a spy.

12 Why do Max and Marcel disagree with Janine about the killing of Sedge?

13 Explain the telephone call Max makes to the Germans at the end of the play.

14 What part of the play keeps you most in suspense?

15 Describe how this suspense is created.